aftermath

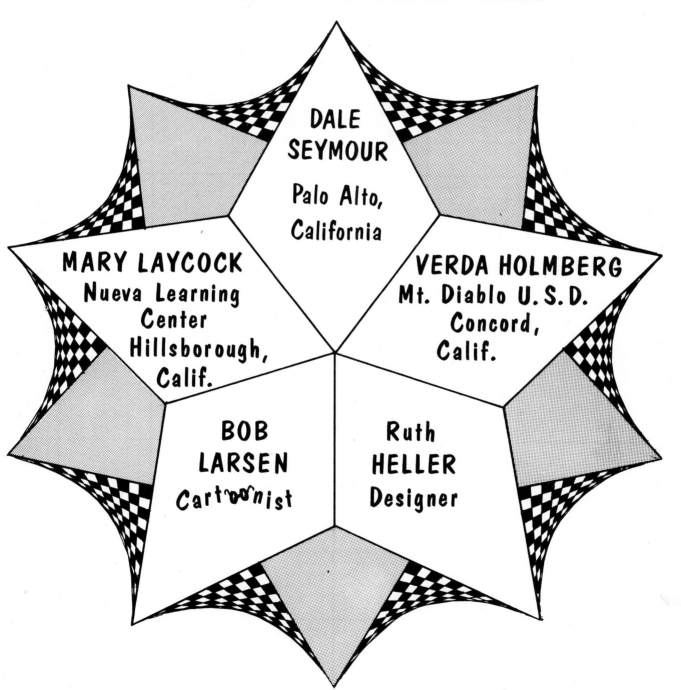

DALE SEYMOUR
Palo Alto, California

MARY LAYCOCK
Nueva Learning Center
Hillsborough, Calif.

VERDA HOLMBERG
Mt. Diablo U.S.D.
Concord, Calif.

BOB LARSEN
Cartoonist

Ruth HELLER
Designer

ISBN: 0-88488-036-2

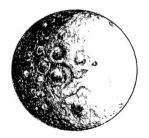

Embark with us on an Expedition to Encounter Exciting Exploratory Experiences.

A PUZZLE PAGE FOR TEACHERS

WHAT IS THE ANSWER TO THESE QUESTIONS?*

a. HOW CAN I PROMOTE STUDENT CREATIVITY IN THE MATH REALM?

f. CAN I EVER CONVINCE STUDENTS THAT MATH IS FUN?

t. HOW CAN I PRODUCTIVELY INVOLVE STUDENTS WHO HAVE FINISHED WITHOUT TEACHING A FRESH LESSON?

e. I AM BORED! IT'S NO WONDER MY STUDENTS ARE, WE ALL NEED A CHANGE OF PACE.

r. HOW CAN I REINFORCE THE REGULAR CURRICULUM IN AN INTERESTING WAY?

a. HOW CAN I GET STUDENTS REGULARLY INVOLVED IN PROBLEM SOLVING?

m. HOW CAN I MEET THE NEEDS OF THE WIDE RANGE OF ABILITIES IN MY MATH CLASS?

h. LOTS OF STUDENTS TURN OFF AT PROBLEM SOLVING BECAUSE IT'S SO WORDY. ISN'T THERE A NON-VERBAL APPROACH SOMEWHERE?

t. DOESN'T ANYBODY MAKE READY-MADE LEARNING CENTERS?

* TO FIND THE ANSWER, ORDER THE LETTERS BY THE QUESTIONS TO FORM ONE WORD.

OKAY... NOW HOW DO I AFTERMATH?

DEDICATION:

THIS BOOK IS
DEDICATED TO COL.
ROBERT S. BEARD. HIS
INSIGHTS INTO THE BEAUTY
OF MATHEMATICS HAVE BEEN
A GREAT INSPIRATION TO
THE AUTHORS OF THIS
BOOK AS WELL AS
MANY OTHERS.

ACKNOWLEDGEMENTS:

JUDY WILLIAMSON

REUBEN SCHADLER

DENNIS HOLMAN

CAROL CASHIN

FRAN WUNDER

FRED HORNBRUCH

BILL JUAREZ

ONE FAIR FRIDAY IN FRANCE, FIVE FEARLESS FELLOWS FORSOOK THE FREEWAYS TO FIND HOW FAST THEIR FERRARI'S FLEW.

THEIR CARS WERE ...

THEIR HELMETS WERE ALSO...

BUT NO DRIVER HAD A CAR WITH THE SAME COLOR OR DECORATION AS HIS HELMET.

(THE DRIVER OF THE WHITE CAR DID NOT WEAR A WHITE HELMET, ETC.)

THEIR CARS WERE NUMBERED...

MORE ON THE NEXT PAGE.

1

CAN YOU COMPLETE THIS CHART?

CAR NO.	CAR COLOR OR DECORATION	HELMET COLOR OR DECORATION	FINISH IN THE RACE
1	_____	_____	_____
2	_____	_____	_____
3	_____	_____	_____
4	_____	_____	_____
5	_____	_____	_____

HERE IS THE INFORMATION YOU WILL NEED TO SOLVE THIS PUZZLE.

1. NO CAR FINISHED THE RACE IN A PLACE THAT CORRESPONDS TO ITS NUMBER.
(CAR NO. 1 DID NOT FINISH 1st, CAR NO. 2 DID NOT FINISH 2nd, ETC.)

2. CAR  DID NOT FINISH IN THE FIRST 3 PLACES.

3. THE DRIVER WEARING WON THE RACE.

4. 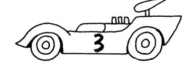 WAS  ()

5. FINISHED BEHIND

2

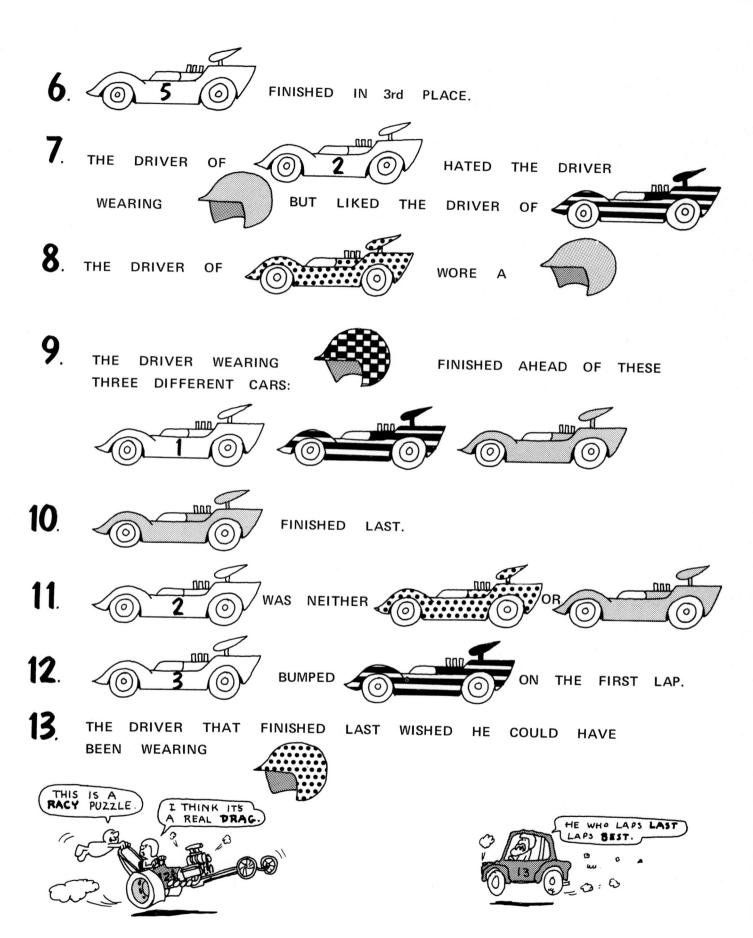

6. [car #5] FINISHED IN 3rd PLACE.

7. THE DRIVER OF [helmet] WEARING [car #2] HATED THE DRIVER BUT LIKED THE DRIVER OF [striped car]

8. THE DRIVER OF [polka-dot car] WORE A [helmet]

9. THE DRIVER WEARING [checkered helmet] FINISHED AHEAD OF THESE THREE DIFFERENT CARS: [car #1] [striped car] [gray car]

10. [gray car] FINISHED LAST.

11. [car #2] WAS NEITHER [polka-dot car] OR [gray car]

12. [car #3] BUMPED [striped car] ON THE FIRST LAP.

13. THE DRIVER THAT FINISHED LAST WISHED HE COULD HAVE BEEN WEARING [polka-dot helmet]

THIS IS A **RACY** PUZZLE.

I THINK IT'S A REAL **DRAG**.

HE WHO LAPS **LAST** LAPS **BEST**.

3

ABCD
EFGH
IND
THE
AREAS.
IJKLM

4

AREA AND PERIMETERS

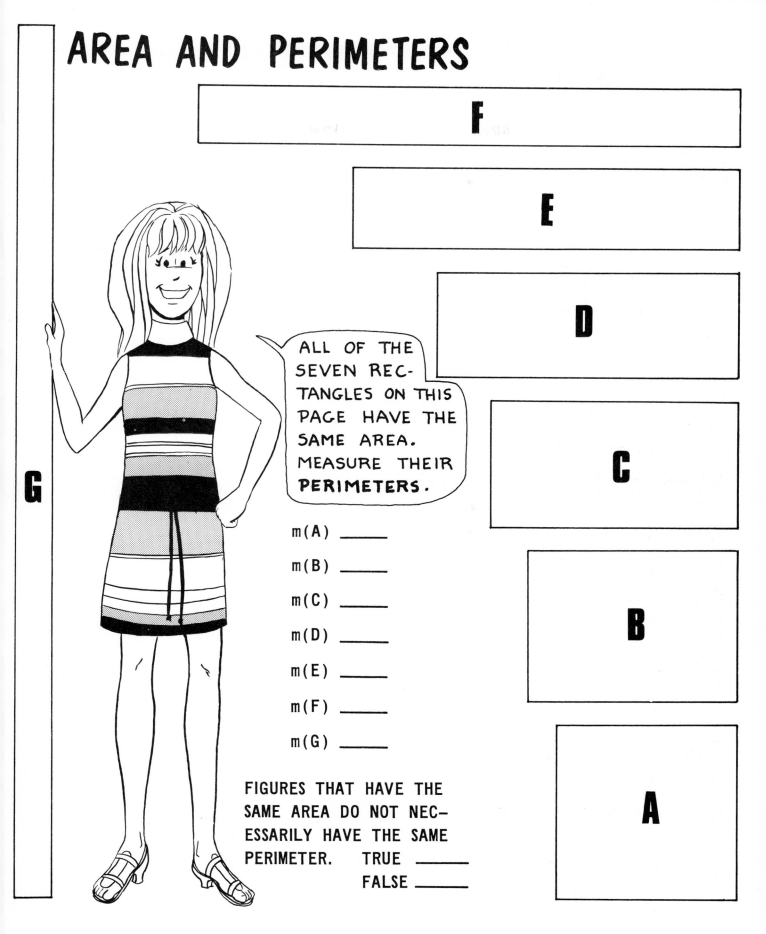

ALL OF THE SEVEN REC-TANGLES ON THIS PAGE HAVE THE SAME AREA. MEASURE THEIR **PERIMETERS.**

m(A) _____

m(B) _____

m(C) _____

m(D) _____

m(E) _____

m(F) _____

m(G) _____

FIGURES THAT HAVE THE SAME AREA DO NOT NEC-ESSARILY HAVE THE SAME PERIMETER.   TRUE _____

FALSE _____

COIN CAPERS

6

MOVING MATCHES

I. REMOVE FOUR MATCHES TO LEAVE ONLY FOUR EQUILATERAL TRIANGLES.

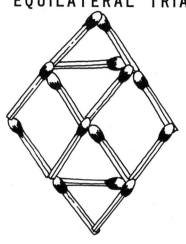

II. MOVE TWO MATCHES TO FORM A TRUE EQUATION.

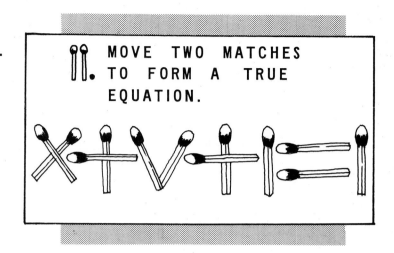

III. 24 MATCHES:

REMOVE FOUR TO MAKE FIVE SQUARES.

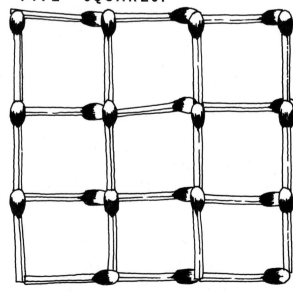

IV. 21 MATCH GAME:

TWO PEOPLE PLAY THIS GAME. LAY OUT 21 MATCHES. PLAYERS TAKE TURNS. DURING A TURN A PLAYER TAKES EITHER ONE, TWO OR THREE MATCHES. THE ONE WHO IS LEFT WITH THE LAST MATCH IS THE LOSER.

MAGIC SQUARE

CAN YOU ARRANGE THE NUMBERS FROM ONE THROUGH NINE IN THIS SQUARE, SO THAT ALL THE COLUMNS AND ROWS, AND EACH OF THE DIAGONALS WILL ADD UP TO THE SAME NUMBER?

UNSCRAMBLE THE SEVEN MATH WORDS BELOW, WRITING EACH IN ITS SPECIAL BOX. TRANSFER THE LETTERS IN THE NUMBERED SQUARES TO THE BLANKS IN THE JOKE AT THE RIGHT!

MATH PUN FUN!

THE DECODED WORD IS THE KEY WORD IN THIS MATH PUN!

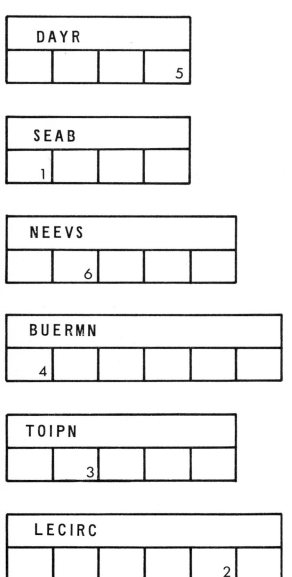

DAYR ☐☐☐☐ 5

SEAB ☐☐☐☐ 1

NEEVS ☐☐☐☐☐ 6

BUERMN ☐☐☐☐☐☐ 4

TOIPN ☐☐☐☐☐ 3

LECIRC ☐☐☐☐☐☐ 2

TAMSTAMIHEC ☐☐☐☐☐☐☐☐☐☐☐ 7

I HEAR YOUR BROTHER IS GOING TO BUSINESS SCHOOL!

YES, FRED IS VERY INTERESTED IN STOCKS AND

___ ___ ___ ___ ___ ___ ___
 1   2   3   4   5   6   7

I WONDER HOW MUCH HOMEWORK IS INVOLVED!

9

TILE TRIAL

HOW MANY PROBLEMS CAN YOU SOLVE BELOW? USE EACH OF THESE FIVE TILES AND ANY COMBINATION OF +, −, X, ÷ SYMBOLS.

EXAMPLE:

$\langle 13 \rangle + \langle 12 \rangle - \langle 10 \rangle - \langle 4 \rangle - \langle 1 \rangle = 10$

5
⬡ ⬡ ⬡ ⬡ ⬡ = **5**

1
⬡ ⬡ ⬡ ⬡ ⬡ = **1**

6
⬡ ⬡ ⬡ ⬡ ⬡ = **6**

2
⬡ ⬡ ⬡ ⬡ ⬡ = **2**

7
⬡ ⬡ ⬡ ⬡ ⬡ = **7**

3
⬡ ⬡ ⬡ ⬡ ⬡ = **3**

8
⬡ ⬡ ⬡ ⬡ ⬡ = **8**

4
⬡ ⬡ ⬡ ⬡ ⬡ = **4**

IT MAY BE HELPFUL TO WRITE THE FIVE NUMBERS ON SCRAPS OF PAPER.

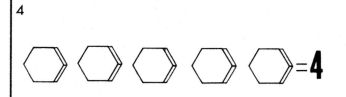

STAR SEARCH

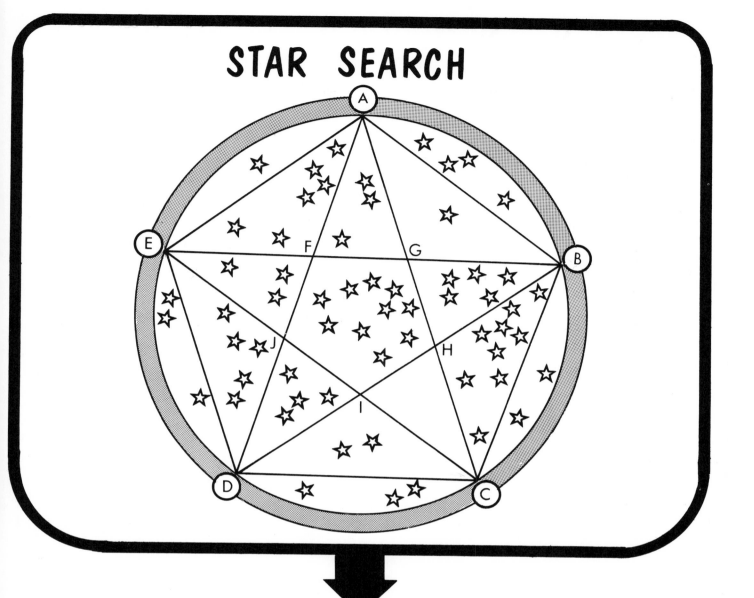

HOW MANY STARS ARE THERE

1. COMMON TO △ EBD AND △ ABH? 5
2. COMMON TO △ ADC AND △ ABD? 10
3. COMMON TO △ BCH AND △ BIC? 9
4. COMMON TO △ EAD AND △ BEC? 3
5. COMMON TO ⬠ ABCDE AND ⬠ FGHIJ? 10
6. COMMON TO THE ◯ AND △ HCD?
7. COMMON TO △ EDC, △ EBD AND △ AED?
8. COMMON TO △ EAB AND △ EBD?

LARGEST NUMBERS?

$99^9 = 99 \times 99 \times 99 \times 99 \times 99 \times 99 \times \_\_ \times \_\_ \times \_\_ .$

ALMOST 100^9 OR 1,000,000,000 — WHICH IS ONE BILLION.

$99^9 = 9387,420,489 = \qquad ?$

IT IS A NUMBER SO LARGE THAT IF PRINTED 16 FIGURES TO THE INCH, IT WOULD FILL 33 VOLUMES OF 800 PAGES WITH 14,000 FIGURES PER PAGE.

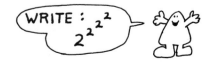

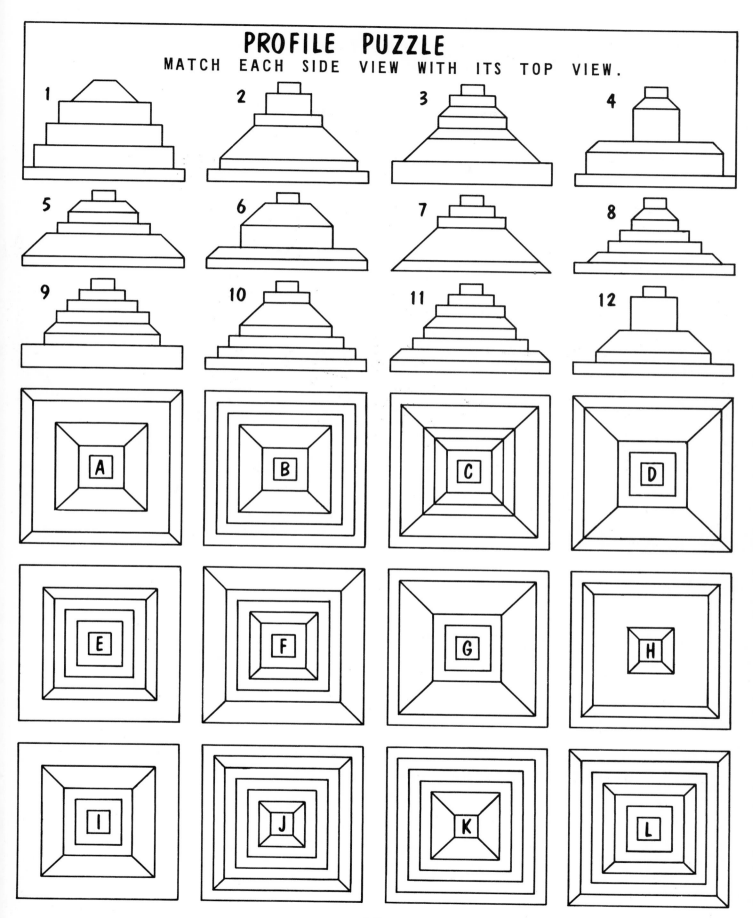

PROFILE PUZZLE
MATCH EACH SIDE VIEW WITH ITS TOP VIEW.

AN ANCIENT MATHEMATICAL GENIUS

"GIVE ME A PLACE TO STAND ___(1)___ ND I'LL MOVE THE EARTH," HE PROCLAIMED.

HE IS CREDITED WITH DISCOVERING THIS SPI ___(2)___ AL.

HE DEVISED METHODS FOR FINDING THE ___(3)___ ENTER OF GRAVITY OF PLANE AND SOLID FIGURES.

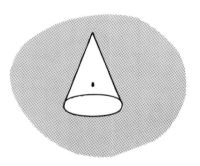

HE DEVISED A CATAPULT WHICH WAS USED TO ___(4)___ EAVE BOULDERS INTO AN ENEMY CAMP.

HE FIGURED THE VALUE OF PI BY SUMMING ___(5)___ NFINITE SERIES.

HE SET AN ENEMY CAMP ON FIRE BY USING A CURVED ___(6)___ IRROR REFLECTING THE SUN'S RAYS.

HE HAD A GENIUS FOR CONSTRUCTING MECHANICAL DEVICES LIKE THE HELICAL SCR (7) W WHICH LIFTED WATER.

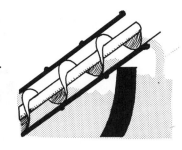

HE SHOUTED "EUREKA" WHEN HE (8) ISCOVERED A WAY TO DETECT IF THE KING'S CROWN WAS SOLID GOLD. (HE WAS TAKING A BATH AT THE TIME.)

HE WAS SLAIN BY A ROMAN SOLDIER BECAUSE H (9) REFUSED TO STOP WORKING ON A PROBLEM.

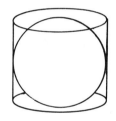

ON HIS TOMB ARE INSCRIBED THE CYLINDER AND (10) PHERE. HE FOUND THE RATIO OF THEIR VOLUMES.

287-212 B.C.

$\overline{1}$ $\overline{2}$ $\overline{3}$ $\overline{4}$ $\overline{5}$ $\overline{6}$ $\overline{7}$ $\overline{8}$ $\overline{9}$ $\overline{10}$

WANTED

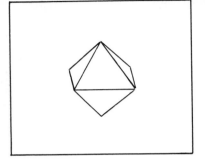

THIS FIGURE IS AN

OCTAHEDRON

IT HAS 8 FACES. ALL OF ITS FACES ARE REGULAR TRIANGLES.

WHAT A FACE!

FOR EACH FACE OF AN OCTAHEDRON THERE IS A FACE DIRECTLY OPPOSITE IT.

THE SIX DRAWINGS SHOWN BELOW ARE ALL DIFFERENT VIEWS OF THE SAME OCTAHEDRON.

WHICH FACE LIES DIRECTLY OPPOSITE

FACE 1? _____   FACE 4? _____   FACE 7? _____

FACE 2? _____   FACE 5? _____   FACE 8? _____

FACE 3? _____   FACE 6? _____

QUILT QUIZ

CUT OUT THE SEVEN HEXAGONAL PUZZLE PIECES AND FIT THEM IN THIS BORDER. WHEN COMPLETED, THE PUZZLE SHOULD BE FORMED BY HEXAGONAL SHAPES OF SIMPLE DESIGN.

I'M A NUMBER GAME

I AM A PRIME TWO DIGIT NUMBER. THE SUM OF MY DIGITS IS DIVISIBLE BY 4. THE PRODUCT OF MY DIGITS IS LESS THAN 5.
WHO AM I ?

I AM A PROPER FRACTION. MY NUMERATOR IS THE NEXT TO SMALLEST PRIME NUMBER . . . MY DENOMINATOR IS THE SMALLEST TWO DIGIT PALINDROMIC NUMBER.
WHAT'S MY NAME ?

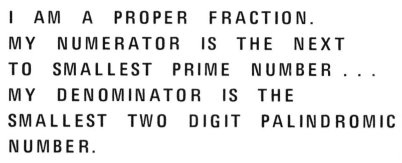

MISSING NUMBERS BUREAU

I AM DIVISIBLE BY FIVE . . . LESS THAN FOUR DIGITS . . . THE SUM OF MY DIGITS IS A SQUARE NUMBER . . . I AM ODD . . . I AM GREATER THAN 12 x 12 . . . THE PRODUCT OF MY DIGITS IS 15. FIND ME !

I AM THE SMALLEST THREE DIGIT SQUARE NUMBER WHOSE DIGITS TOTAL A NUMBER THAT IS NOT A SQUARE. WHO AM I?

AMNESIA WARD

I AM A COUNTING NUMBER. ALL THREE OF MY DIGITS ARE EVEN BUT DIFFERENT. I AM DIVISIBLE BY 4 . . . THE SUM OF MY DIGITS IS 12. THE SUM OF MY UNITS AND TENS DIGITS EQUALS MY HUNDREDS DIGIT.

I AM LESS THAN THE PRODUCT OF THE FOURTH AND FIFTH TRIANGULAR NUMBERS . . . I AM GREATER THAN THE TWELFTH SQUARE NUMBER . . . I AM DIVISIBLE BY SEVEN . . . CAN YOU FIND ME?

PROPORTIONAL DRAWING

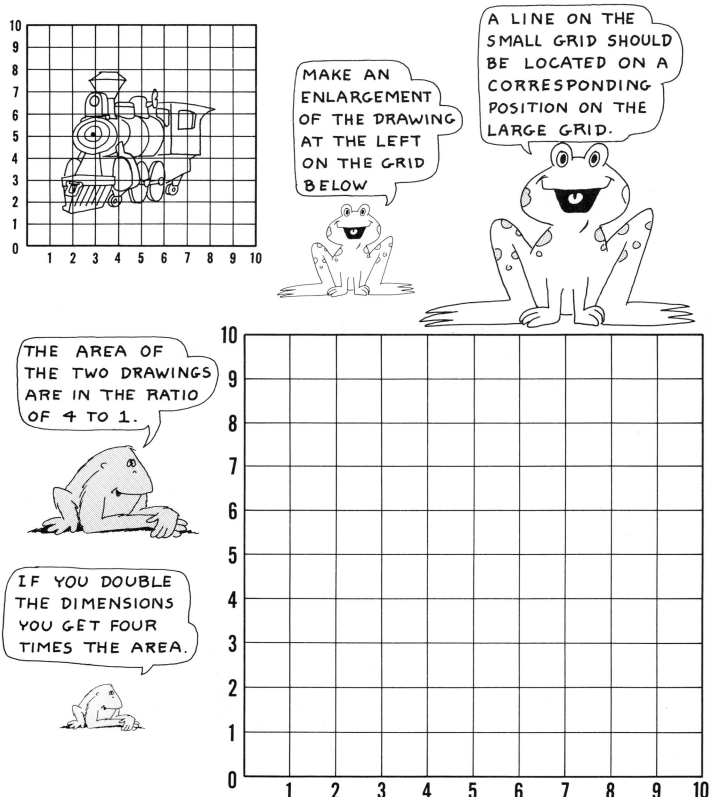

MAKE AN ENLARGEMENT OF THE DRAWING AT THE LEFT ON THE GRID BELOW

A LINE ON THE SMALL GRID SHOULD BE LOCATED ON A CORRESPONDING POSITION ON THE LARGE GRID.

THE AREA OF THE TWO DRAWINGS ARE IN THE RATIO OF 4 TO 1.

IF YOU DOUBLE THE DIMENSIONS YOU GET FOUR TIMES THE AREA.

SUM DECIMALS

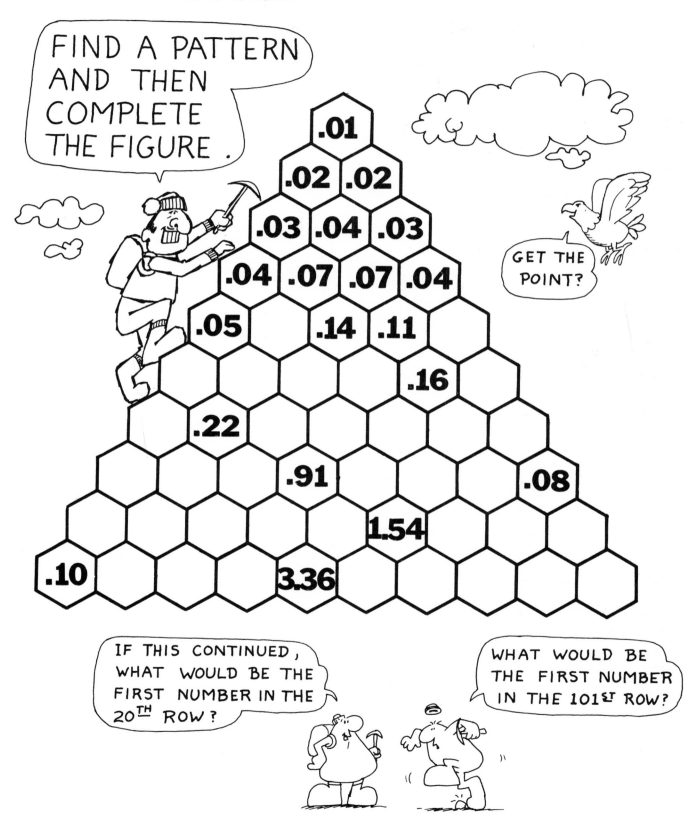

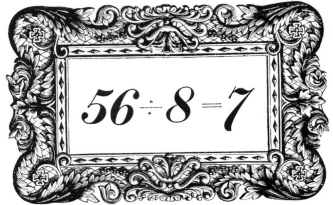

$$56 \div 8 = 7$$

Ye olde math

LESSON I.

DIVISION is finding how many times one number or quantity is contained in another : thus,

1. How many churches will three bells supply, if each church has one bell ?

One is contained in three how many times ?

2. If one man can make 2 axes in one day, how many days will it take him to make 4 axes ?

Two is contained in four how many times ?

3. A lady gave 6 dolls to some children, giving them 2 apiece ; to how many children did she give the dolls ?

Two is contained in six how many times ?

4. If a chair-maker can make 3 chairs in a day, how many days will it take him to make 9 chairs ?

Three is contained in nine how many times ?

5. James gave 8 bunches of grapes to his sisters, giving them 4 bunches each ; how many sisters had he ?

Four is contained in eight how many times ?

22

141. Divide 14378 by 170.

1ST OPERATION.

```
170) 1437|8 (84
      136
      ‾‾‾
       77
       68
      ‾‾‾
       98, Rem.
```

2D OPERATION.

```
17Ø) 1437.8 (84.576+
      136
      ‾‾‾
       77
       68
      ‾‾‾
       98
       85
      ‾‾‾
      130
      119
      ‾‾‾
      110
      102
      ‾‾‾
        8
```

Dividing both divisor and dividend by 10, we have in the dividend 1437 and 8 remainder. Dividing 1437 by 17, we have 84 and 9 tens remainder. Adding the two remainders, the 9 tens and the 8 units, together, we have 98 as the full remainder.

In this operation we have divided both divisor and dividend by 10, as in Ex. 139, and then continued the division to thousandths. As there is still a remainder, we write + at the right of the quotient.

PRIME PATTERN

COMPLETE THE SPIRAL OF NUMBERS AND SHADE EACH SQUARE THAT CONTAINS A PRIME. NOTICE "STRINGS" OF PRIMES AND COMPOSITES ALONG DIAGONAL LINES!

RATIO

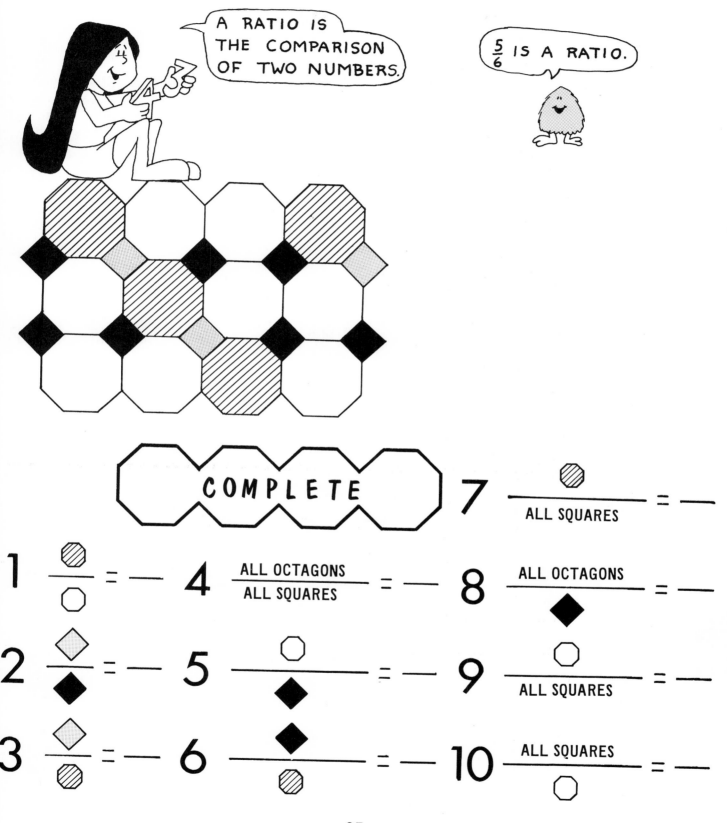

FACES OR VASES

1) ARE THE BASES OF THE SQUARES IN ONE ROW PARALLEL?
2) WHICH CENTER CIRCLES ARE LARGER?
3) DO YOU SEE FACES OR VASES?

A WHOLE THING

IF THE MEASURE OF THE
SHADED REGION IS ONE, THEN
FIND THE MEASURE OF THE:

1a) DOTTED REGION

1b) STRIPED REGION

1c) CROSSED REGION

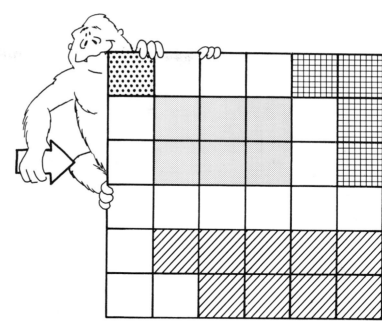

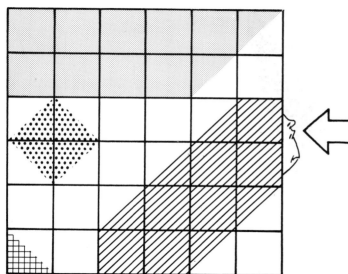

IF THE MEASURE OF THE
SHADED REGION IS ONE, THEN
FIND THE MEASURE OF THE:

2a) DOTTED REGION

2b) STRIPED REGION

2c) CROSSED REGION

IF THE MEASURE OF THE
CROSSED REGION IS 1/2, THEN
FIND THE MEASURE OF THE:

3a) DOTTED REGION

3b) SHADE IN A REGION THAT
REPRESENTS 1

3c) STRIPE IN A REGION WHICH
REPRESENTS 2/7

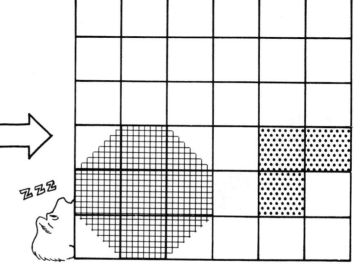

BASE FOURTEEN

CODE

X	0	I	5	T	10
E	1	N	6	U	11
F	2	O	7	V	12
G	3	R	8	W	13
H	4	S	9		

IN BASE FOURTEEN, WHICH IS LARGEST TWO OR SIX?

YOU CAN'T BELIEVE A WORD OF IT!

IS ONE + ONE = TWO?

SINCE 2 4 6 8,
IS TWO   FOUR   SIX   EIGHT?

TWO   10 (196) + 13 (14) + 7 = 2149

FOUR   2 (__) + 7 (__) + 11 (__) + 8 =

SIX   _____ + _____ + _____ =

EIGHT _____ + _____ + _____ + _____ + _____ =

THIS MAY HELP!

14^4	14^3	14^2	14^1	14^0
(38,416)	(2,744)	(196)	14	1

A WHOLE THING

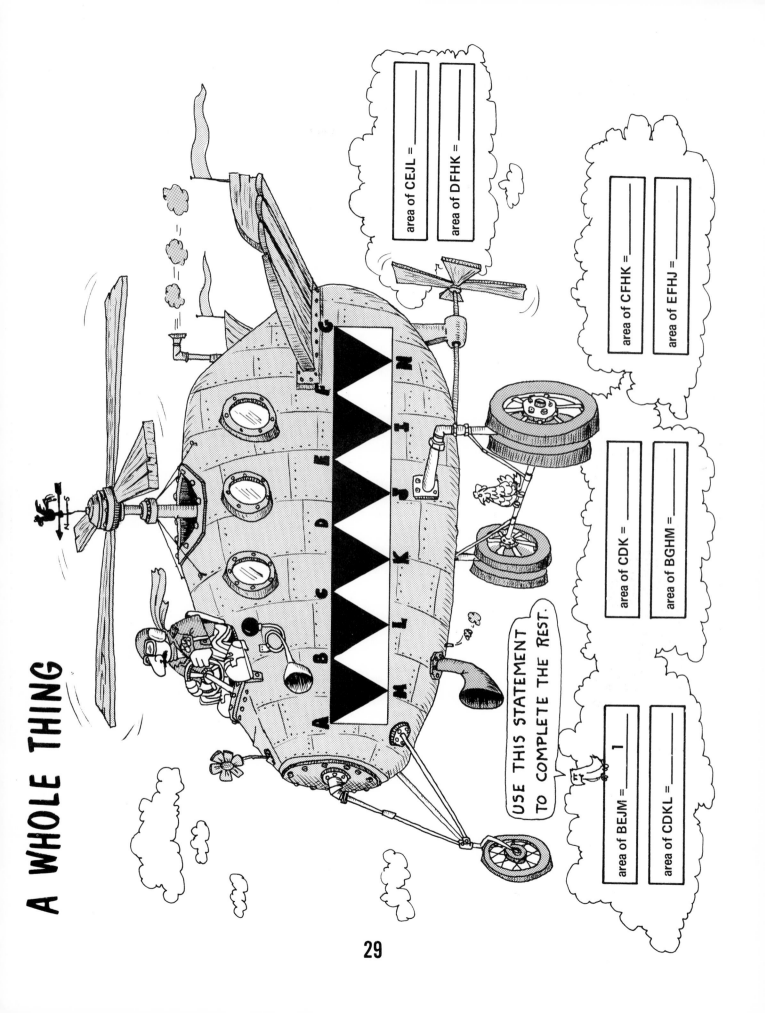

area of CEJL = _____

area of DFHK = _____

area of CFHK = _____

area of EFHJ = _____

area of CDK = _____

area of BGHM = _____

USE THIS STATEMENT TO COMPLETE THE REST.

area of BEJM = 1

area of CDKL = _____

DOMINO FACTORY MAZE

SUE SCHMICK HAD AN AFTER SCHOOL JOB IN A DOMINO FACTORY. SHE DESIGNED THE FRACTION MAZE WHERE EACH DOMINO REPRESENTS A FRACTION. THE SMALLER NUMBER IN EACH CASE REPRESENTS THE NUMERATOR, SO THERE ARE NO FRACTIONS GREATER THAN ONE. MOVE FROM THE START TO FINISH, ALTERNATELY ADDING TWO DOMINOES AND SUBTRACTING TWO DOMINOES.

ADD-SUB SLIDE RULE

HERE IS A SLIDE RULE YOU CAN MAKE TO HELP YOU ADD AND SUBTRACT **INTEGERS**.

FIRST: CUT OUT SLIDE A AND FOLDER B.

| -7 | -6 | -5 | -4 | -3 | -2 | -1 | 0 | +1 | +2 | +3 | +4 | +5 | +6 | +7 |

ADD-SUB INTEGERS

SLIDE A

| -7 | -6 | -5 | -4 | -3 | -2 | -1 | 0 | +1 | +2 | +3 | +4 | +5 | +6 | +7 |

- -

FOLD ON DOTTED LINE

FOLDER B

SECOND: FOLD BACK FOLDER B ON THE DOTTED LINE.

THIRD: PLACE A INSIDE FOLDER B.   THE NUMBER LINE ON A APPEARS ABOVE THE NUMBER LINE ON B.

ON THE NEXT PAGE WE WILL SHOW YOU HOW TO USE THIS SLIDE RULE.

ADD-SUB SLIDE RULE

PROBLEM: $^-2 + {}^+4 = N$

1. PULL SLIDE **A** UNTIL **0** IS OVER **−2** ON FOLDER **B**.

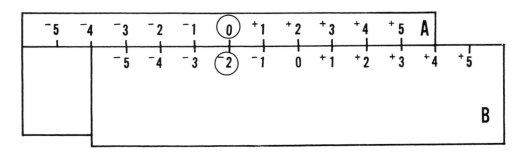

2. ON SLIDE **A** FIND **⁺4**. THE ANSWER, **N**, IS UNDER **⁺4**.

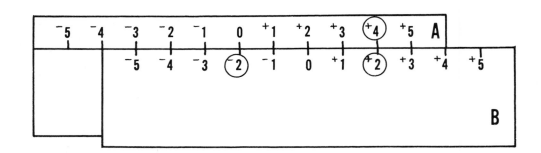

TRY THESE PROBLEMS ON THE
ADD-SUB SLIDE RULE:

$^+3 + {}^-4 = N$ $\qquad$ $^+6 + {}^-4 = N$

$^-1 + {}^-5 = N$ $\qquad$ $^-7 + {}^+7 = N$

$^-4 + 0 = N$ $\qquad$ $^-4 + {}^-1 = N$

$^-6 + {}^+6 = N$ $\qquad$ $^-2 + {}^-5 = N$

(CONTINUED)

32

ADD-SUB SLIDE RULE

HERE'S HOW TO SUBTRACT INTEGERS ON THE ADD-SUB SLIDE RULE.

PROBLEM: $^-3 - ^-6 = N$

1. PULL THE SLIDE A UNTIL 0 IS OVER −6 ON B.

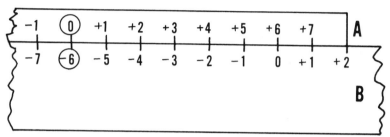

2. THINK: WHAT SEGMENT ON A IS NEEDED TO ARRIVE AT −3 ON B? YOUR ANSWER IS DIRECTLY ABOVE −3 ON B. N=_____

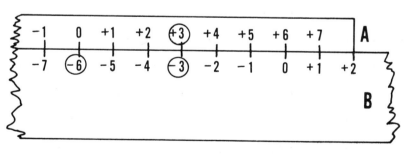

TRY THESE SUBTRACTION PROBLEMS ON THE ADD−SUB SLIDE RULE.

$^+2 - ^-2 = N$

$^+5 - ^+5 = N$

$^-7 - ^-2 = N$

$^-1 - ^+6 = N$

$^-4 - 0 = N$

─THAT'S ALL!

33

INTEGERS

-3-2-10234

THE TABLE BELOW CONTAINS MANY PATTERNS. SEE IF YOU CAN COMPLETE IT AND DIS—COVER RULES FOR INTEGERS.

+	-6	-5	-4	-3	-2	-1	0	1	2	3	4	5	6
-6										-3	-2		
-5										-2	-1		
-4	-10	-9	-8	-7	-6	-5	-4	-3	-2	-1	0	1	2
-3										0	1		
-2										1	2		
-1										2	3		
0							0	1	2	3	4	5	6
1							1	2	3	4		6	7
2							2	3	4	5	6	7	8
3							3	4	5	6	7	8	9
4							4	5	6	7	8	9	10
5	-1	0	1	2	3	4	5	6	7	8	9	10	11
6							6	7	8	9	10	11	12

1) POSITIVE + POSITIVE = _____

2) 3 + 5 = _____

3) POSITIVE + NEGATIVE = _____

4) -3 + 5 = _____

5) -9 + 4 = _____

6) -6 + 6 = _____

7) NEGATIVE + NEGATIVE = _____

8) -7 + (-5) = _____

AN INTEGERESTING PROBLEM.

34

INTEGERS

USE PATTERNS TO HELP YOU COMPLETE THIS MULTIPLICATION TABLE FOR **INTEGERS**.

1) POSITIVE x POSITIVE = _____
2)   5 x 6 = _____
3) POSITIVE x NEGATIVE = _____
4)   −5 x −6 = _____
5)   3 x (−4) = _____
6) NEGATIVE x NEGATIVE = _____
7)   −4 x (−5) = _____

x	−6	−5	−4	−3	−2	−1	0	1	2	3	4	5	6
−6											-24		
−5	30	25	20	15	10	5	0	-5	-10	-15	-20	-25	-30
−4											-16		
−3											-12		
−2											-8		
−1											-4		
0							0	0	0	0	0	0	0
1							0	1	2	3	4	5	6
2							0	2	4	6	8	10	12
3	-18	-15	-12	-9	-6	-3	0	3	6	9	12	15	18
4							0	4	8	12	16	20	24
5							0	5	10	15	20	25	30
6							0	6	12	18	24	30	36

DECODE THIS MESSAGE IN THE LARGE SQUARE

up	to	filled	word.	message	up	to
a	is	last	This	move	a	is
place	the	decoded	you	If	place	the
below	be	if	right.	the	below	be
can	and	the	place	word	can	and
up	to	filled	word.	message	up	to
a	is	last	This	move	a	is

36

LINE DESIGN

START AT 1 (BIG NUMERALS) AND CONNECT 1 WITH 2, 2 WITH 4, 3 WITH 6, 4 WITH 8, AND SO ON, CONNECTING EACH NUMBER WITH ITS DOUBLE. NEXT, START WITH 1 (SMALL NUMERALS) AND DO THE SAME. THE RESULTING SHAPE IS CALLED A CARDIOID.

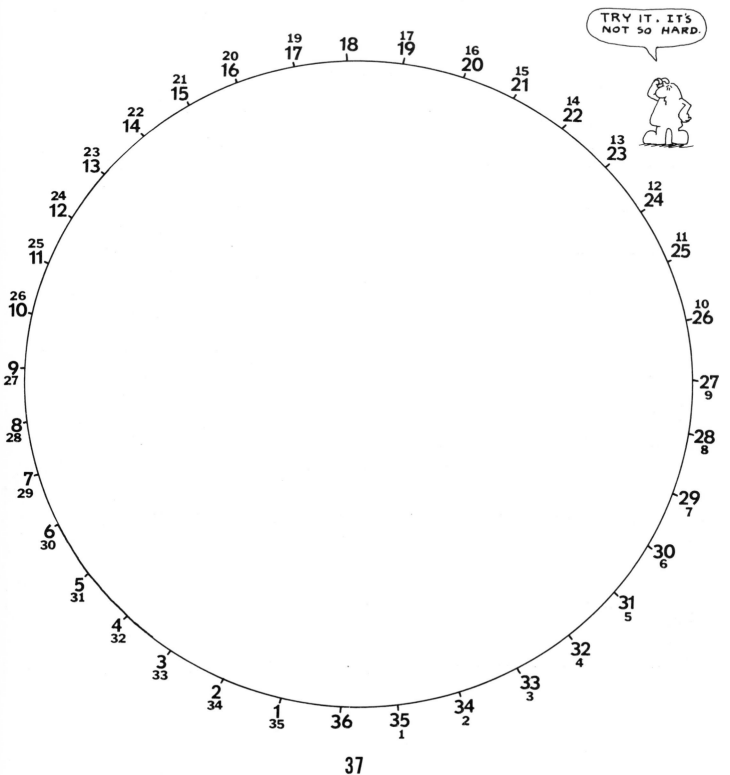

TRY IT. IT'S NOT SO HARD.

37

ROCK TALK

THE **GREEN TOMATOES** ROCK GROUP HAS FOUR MEMBERS: **BOB**, **DENNY**, **GIL**, AND **PETE**. THEY PLAY THE **BASS**, **DRUMS**, **GUITAR** AND **PIANO**. NO ONE PLAYS AN INSTRUMENT THAT BEGINS WITH THE SAME LETTER AS HIS FIRST NAME. **BOB** HATES THE PIANO PLAYER. **PETE** AND THE DRUMMER ARE BEST FRIENDS. **GIL** PLAYS THE **BASS** WHICH HE BORROWED FROM **BOB**. WHICH INSTRUMENT DOES EACH PERSON PLAY?

ARROWMATH ➡

CAN YOU SOLVE THESE **ARROWMATH** PROBLEMS ?

EXAMPLES :

$5 \rightarrow = 10$

$5 \searrow = 6$

$15 \nearrow = 11$

Hexagon grid:

5	10	15	20	23
6	11	16	21
2	7	12	17	22
3	8	13	18
1	4	9	14	19

SOLVE :

(1) $8 \rightarrow =$ _____

(2) $13 \nearrow =$ _____

(3) $8 \searrow \nearrow =$ _____

(4) $13 \rightarrow \nearrow \leftarrow =$ _____

(5) $11 \rightarrow \rightarrow \nearrow \downarrow \leftarrow =$ _____

(6) $12 \rightarrow \nearrow \searrow \swarrow \rightarrow \nearrow \downarrow \swarrow \downarrow \downarrow \leftarrow \searrow \rightarrow =$ _____

(7) DOES $21 \rightarrow$ HAVE ANY MEANING ?

(8) DOES $4 \uparrow$ OR $\downarrow$ HAVE ANY MEANING ?

(9) WHAT IS THE INVERSE OF $\nearrow$?

(10) DOES $7 \rightarrow 5$ HAVE A MEANING ?

(CONTINUED)

ARROWMATH

HERE ARE SOME NEW DEFINITIONS FOR ARROWMATH ARROWS.

→	MEANS **ADD** THE NUMBER TO THE RIGHT.
←	MEANS **SUBTRACT** THE NUMBER TO THE LEFT.
↗	MEANS **MULTIPLY** THE NUMBER ABOVE AND TO THE RIGHT.
↖	MEANS **DIVIDE** BY THE NUMBER ABOVE AND TO THE LEFT.

EXAMPLES :

$1 \rightarrow = 6$

$1 \leftarrow = -2$

$1 \searrow = \frac{1}{4}$

$1 \nearrow = 12$

$1 \rightarrow \rightarrow = 20$

SOLVE :

① $6 \rightarrow = $ ____

② $6 \rightarrow \rightarrow = $ ____

③ $3 \nearrow \rightarrow = $ ____

④ $15 \rightarrow \leftarrow = $ ____

⑤ $8 \nearrow \rightarrow = $ ____

⑥ $8 \rightarrow \nearrow = $ ____

⑦ $11 \rightarrow \nearrow = $ ____

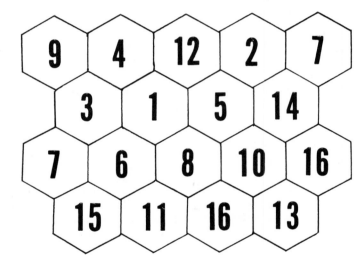

⑧ ARE OPERATIONS ↘ AND ↙ DEFINED ?

⑨ IN PROBLEMS 5 & 6 WAS $8 \nearrow \rightarrow = 8 \rightarrow \nearrow$?

⑩ IS $6 \rightarrow \leftarrow$ EQUAL TO $6 \leftarrow \rightarrow$?

⑪ ARE ← AND → INVERSES ?

⑫ INVENT A MATH SYSTEM OF YOUR OWN AND TRY IT ON YOUR FRIENDS.

WHICH ONE DIFFERS?

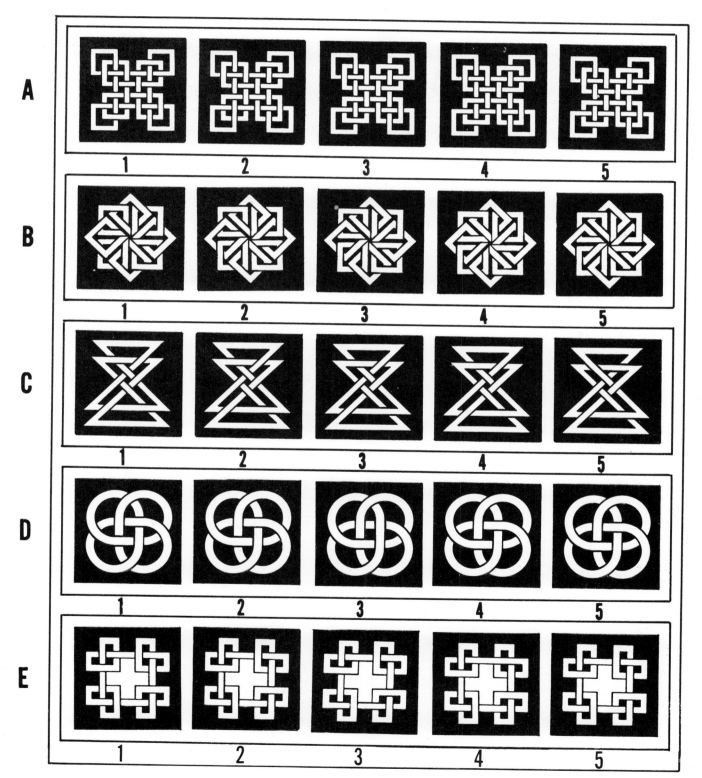

BORDER — 10 HEADS.
CENTER — 2 TAILS.

CAN YOU FIND A NUMBER OF PENNIES (LESS THAN 50) WHERE THE HEADS AND TAILS WOULD BE EQUAL IN THE BORDER AND CENTER?

COIN CAPERS

MAKE THIS

INTO THIS

EACH COIN MOVED MUST TOUCH TWO OTHER COINS.

IF AT FIRST YOU DON'T SUCCEED, TRY TRY AGAIN!

DID YOU COIN THAT PHRASE?

METRIC MEASURE

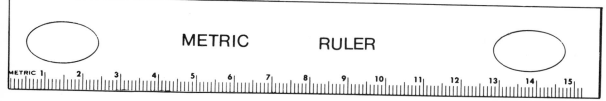

METRIC   RULER

THE RULER SHOWN ABOVE IS A METRIC
RULER. THE RULER IS MARKED OFF IN
CENTIMETRES. EACH CENTIMETRE IS
DIVIDED INTO TEN SMALLER UNITS
CALLED MILLIMETRES. USE A METRIC
RULER TO MEASURE THE LINE SEGMENTS
IN THIS FIGURE.

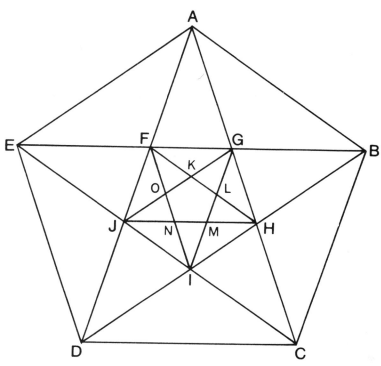

1) m(AB) = ____ mm   OR   ____ cm

2) m(EC) = ____ mm   OR   ____ cm

3) m(DJ) = ____ mm   OR   ____ cm

4) m(GH) = ____ mm   OR   ____ cm

5) m(CG) = ____ mm   OR   ____ cm

6) m(GI) = ____ mm   OR   ____ cm

7) m(LH) = ____ mm   OR   ____ cm

8) m(MN) = ____ mm   OR   ____ cm

9) m(NH) = ____ mm   OR   ____ cm

IT'S EASY TO CHANGE mm TO cm.

43

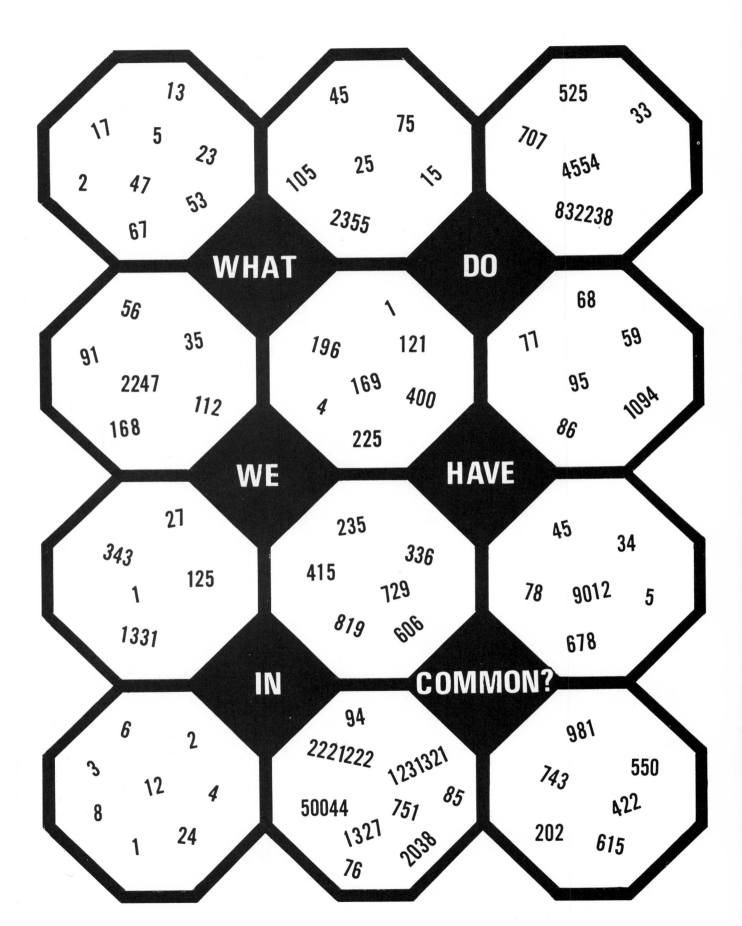

44

AVERAGES

AN AVERAGE IS THE SUM
OF NUMBERS IN A SET,
DIVIDED BY THE NUMBER
OF NUMBERS

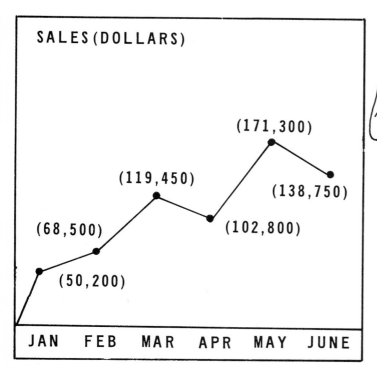

SALES (DOLLARS)

(171,300)

(119,450)

(138,750)

(68,500)

(102,800)

(50,200)

JAN   FEB   MAR   APR   MAY   JUNE

WHAT WERE THE AVERAGE
MONTHLY SALES?

WHAT WAS THE TIGERS'
AVERAGE SCORE?

BASKETBALL

TIGERS	66	—	BEARS	50
TIGERS	58	—	CATS	39
TIGERS	68	—	SNAKES	71
TIGERS	45	—	RABBITS	43
TIGERS	51	—	RATS	62
TIGERS	47	—	OWLS	42
TIGERS	72	—	ANTS	14
TIGERS	37	—	SEALS	78
TIGERS	61	—	YOIKS	60
TIGERS	54	—	ZEEKS	48
TIGERS	57	—	YECHS	10

WHAT WAS THE OPPONENTS'
AVERAGE SCORE?

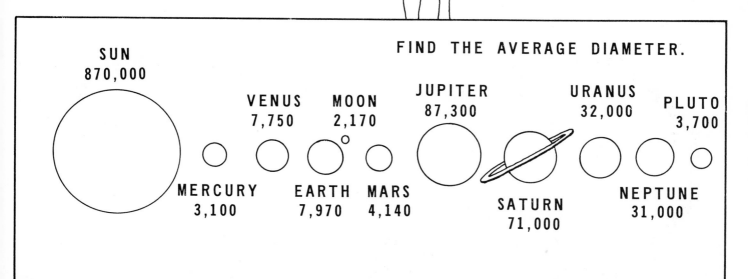

FIND THE AVERAGE DIAMETER.

SUN
870,000

VENUS
7,750

MOON
2,170

JUPITER
87,300

URANUS
32,000

PLUTO
3,700

MERCURY
3,100

EARTH
7,970

MARS
4,140

SATURN
71,000

NEPTUNE
31,000

WHICH ARE NOT CONGRUENT?

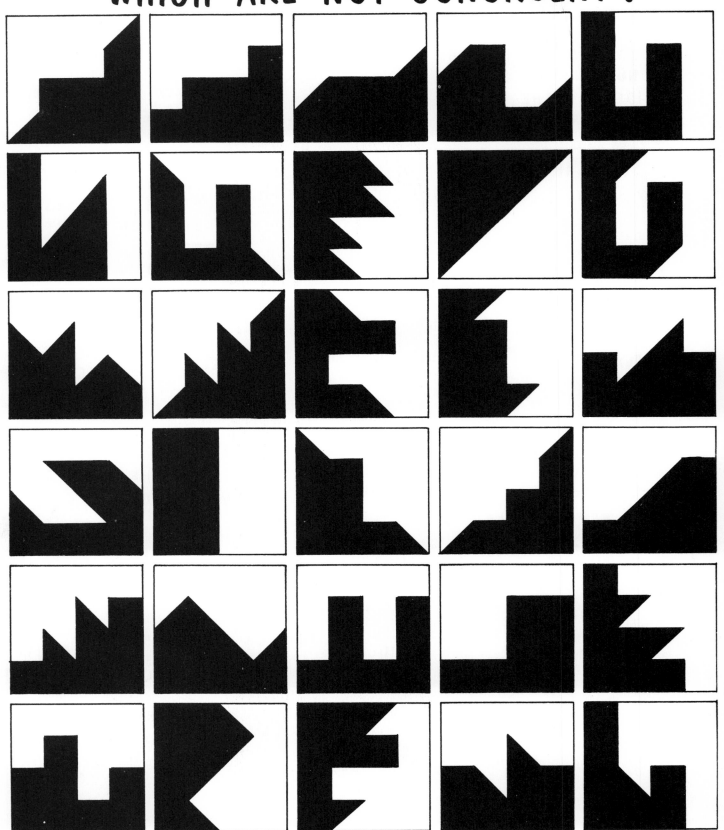

HOW MANY WAYS CAN YOU MAKE CHANGE FOR ME **WITHOUT** USING PENNIES?

WOULD YOU BELIEVE 40?

	5¢	10¢	25¢	50¢
1	___	___	___	___
2	___	___	___	___
3	___	___	___	___
4	___	___	___	___
5	___	___	___	___
6	___	___	___	___
7	___	___	___	___
8	___	___	___	___
9	___	___	___	___
10	___	___	___	___
11	___	___	___	___
12	___	___	___	___
13	___	___	___	___
14	___	___	___	___

	5¢	10¢	25¢	50¢
15	___	___	___	___
16	___	___	___	___
17	___	___	___	___
18	___	___	___	___
19	___	___	___	___
20	___	___	___	___
21	___	___	___	___
22	___	___	___	___
23	___	___	___	___
24	___	___	___	___
25	___	___	___	___
26	___	___	___	___
27	___	___	___	___
28	___	___	___	___

	5¢	10¢	25¢	50¢
29	___	___	___	___
30	___	___	___	___
31	___	___	___	___
32	___	___	___	___
33	___	___	___	___
34	___	___	___	___
35	___	___	___	___
36	___	___	___	___
37	___	___	___	___
38	___	___	___	___
39	___	___	___	___
40	___	___	___	___

HOW MANY WAYS CAN YOU CHANGE A $50 BILL USING 5, 10, AND 20 DOLLAR BILLS?

47

TRACE A PATH TO THE CENTER

GOLDBACH'S CONJECTURE

IN 1742, THE GERMAN MATHEMATICIAN
C. GOLDBACH, MADE THE CONJECTURE
THAT EVERY EVEN NUMBER EXCEPT TWO
WAS THE SUM OF TWO PRIMES.

EVEN NUMBER

PRIME NUMBER

PRIME NUMBER

IN THE FIGURE BELOW, WRITE THE TWO PRIMES
THAT TOTAL THE EVEN NUMBER.

PRIME FACTOR TENTS

USE ALL OF THE NUMBERS TO COMPLETE THESE FACTOR TENTS.

90 94 75 64 76 86 84 96 80 88 87 85 91 78 72

87

3 × 29

WHAT'S MY WORD?

IN THESE PROBLEMS, LETTERS HAVE REPLACED NUMBERS. BY STUDYING THE PROBLEMS, CAN YOU FIND THE **CODE WORD**?

| | 0 | 1 | 2 | 3 | 4 | 5 | 6 | 7 | 8 | 9 |

```
        LON                    SIN                 IS
   T )TIP              H )OPEN            H )THE
      TCC                    OHCC              TOC
      IP                      TEN               OE
      SC                      TOC               OH
      OP                      TN                L
      OP                      TS
                              T
```

```
  NINE
 -TEN
  NETS
```

TEN - ONE = SH

A WHOLE THING

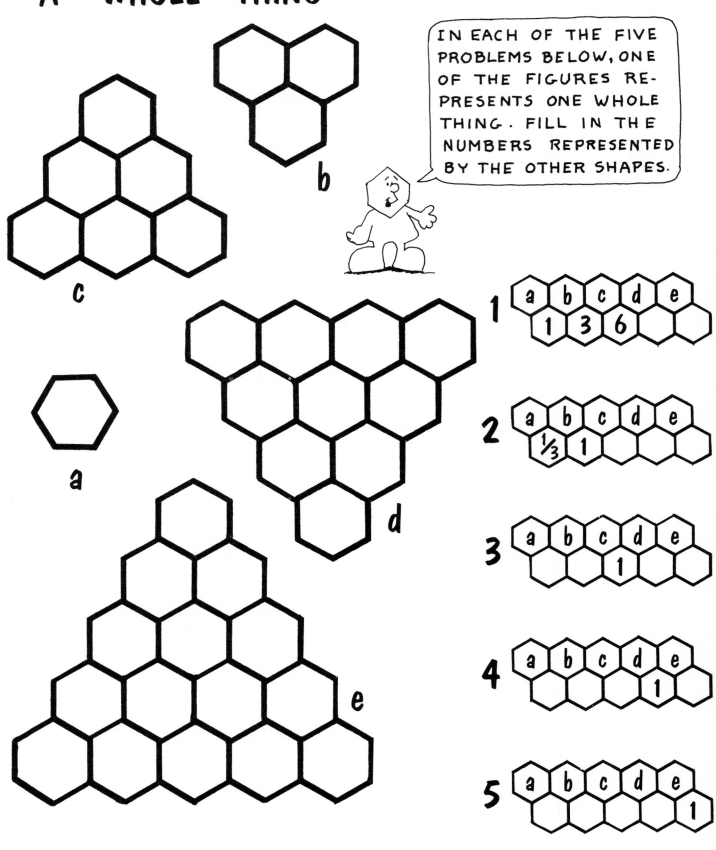

IN EACH OF THE FIVE PROBLEMS BELOW, ONE OF THE FIGURES REPRESENTS ONE WHOLE THING. FILL IN THE NUMBERS REPRESENTED BY THE OTHER SHAPES.

b

c

a

d

e

1 a b c d e
   1 3 6

2 a b c d e
   1/3 1

3 a b c d e
        1

4 a b c d e
        1

5 a b c d e
              1

HOW MANY ?

1.

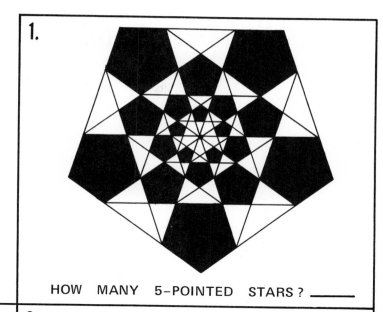

HOW MANY 5-POINTED STARS ? _____

2.

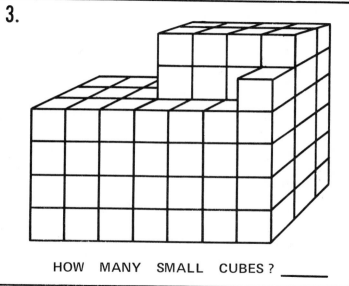

HOW MANY HEXAGONS ? _____

3.

HOW MANY SMALL CUBES ? _____

4.

1 3 5 8

HOW MANY DIFFERENT 3-DIGIT NUMERALS CAN YOU WRITE USING THE NUMERALS SHOWN ABOVE ? _____

53

FRACTION TILE

USE THREE OF THESE FOUR TILES TO MAKE A TRUE NUMBER SENTENCE.

$\frac{1}{2}$ $\frac{1}{3}$ $\frac{1}{6}$ $\frac{1}{4}$

SURF'S UP

1. $\boxed{} - \boxed{} + \boxed{} = \frac{7}{12}$

2. $\boxed{} + \boxed{} - \boxed{} = \frac{5}{12}$

3. $\boxed{} + \boxed{} + \boxed{} = 1$

4. $\boxed{} - \boxed{} - \boxed{} = 0$

5. $\boxed{} + \boxed{} - \boxed{} = \frac{11}{12}$

6. $\boxed{} + \boxed{} - \boxed{} = \frac{1}{12}$

7. $\boxed{} + \boxed{} - \boxed{} = \frac{2}{3}$

8. $\boxed{} + \boxed{} + \boxed{} = \frac{11}{12}$

ONE OF THESE CAN'T BE DONE.

PRETTY SNEAKY.

54

DESI and CAROL....

...WERE PLAYING
5 – IN – A – ROW
USING ORDERED
PAIRS.

CAROL USED X'S AND STARTED FIRST.   THEY MARKED THEIR
X'S AND O'S ON THE INTERSECTIONS OF THE LINES INSTEAD
OF IN THE SQUARES .

PLAY OUT THEIR GAME AND SEE WHAT THEIR GAME SHEET
LOOKED LIKE .

HERE WERE THEIR MOVES IN ORDER :
   (5,6) , (6,7) , (6,6) , (7,6) , (5,5) , (5,8) , (8,5) , (4,9) ,
   (3,10) , (7,8) , (7,7) , (8,8) , (4,4) , (3,3) , (6,8) , (9,8) ,
   (10,8) , (8,7) , (6,5) , (10,9) , (11,10) , (8,9) , (7,5) , (9,5) , (4,5)

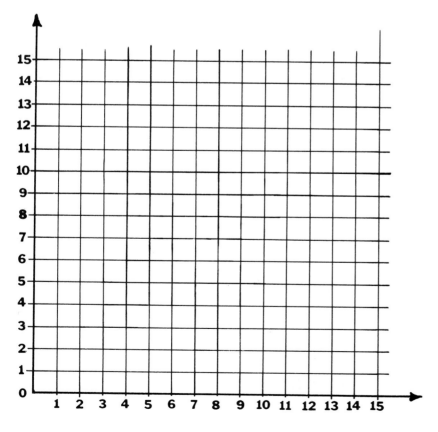

YOU SHOULD BE
COORDINATED
TO PLAY THIS
GAME.

THE MOST PROLIFIC OF THE WORLD'S MATHEMATICIANS.

HE IS CREDITED WITH DISCOVERING THIS FORMULA :

VERTICES + FACES = _(1)_DGES + 2

8 + 6 = 12 + 2

FACE
EDGE
VERTEX

P_(2)_ZZLES LIKE THE SEVEN BRIDGES OF KONINGSBERG INTERESTED HIM AND WERE PART OF THE NEW MATHEMATICS CALLED TOPOLOGY THAT HE STARTED.

HE HAD 13 GRANDCHILDREN AND DIED WHILE PLAYING WITH A GRANDCHILD. HE IS SAID TO HAVE CREATED MATHE-MATICS WITH A BABY ON HIS _(3)_ AP AND CHILDREN PLAYING AROUND.

HE CONTRIBUTED GREATLY TO THE FOUNDATIONS OF EVERY BRANCH OF ADVANCED MATHEMATICS; MOST OF HIS WORK IS TOO DIFFICULT FOR THIS BOOK. THE LETTER NEEDED IS THE FIRST ONE USED IN THREE OF HIS FAMOUS EQUATIONS.

$$e^{i\pi} + 1 = 0$$
$$e = \lim_{n \to \infty} \left(1 + \frac{1}{n}\right)^n$$
$$e = 1 + \frac{1}{1} + \frac{1}{1 \cdot 2} + \frac{1}{1 \cdot 2 \cdot 3} + ..$$

(4)

SO NUMEROUS WERE HIS MATHEMATICAL MANUSCRIPTS THAT 200 VOLUMES WILL BE _(5)_EQUIRED TO ORGANIZE THEM INTO BOOK FORM. HE WROTE 800 PAGES A YEAR OF HIGH QUALITY MATHEMATICS.

1708 - 1783

<u>   </u> <u>   </u> <u>   </u> <u>   </u> <u>   </u>
 1   2   3   4   5

EULER LINES

CAN YOU DRAW EACH DESIGN BELOW WITHOUT CROSSING OR
RETRACING A LINE OR LIFTING THE PENCIL FROM THE PAPER?

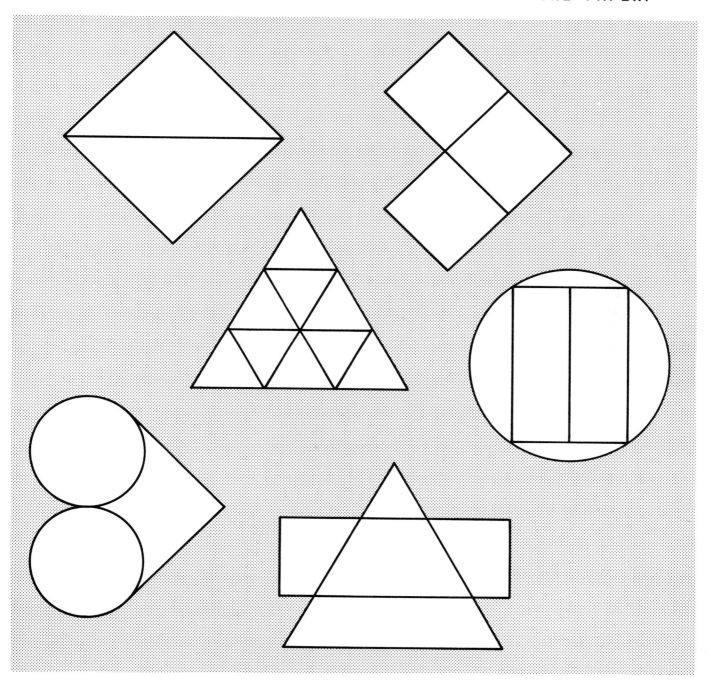

THE SWISS MATHEMATICIAN LEONHARD EULER (PRONOUNCED
OILER) DISCOVERED A GENERAL RULE THAT ONE CAN USE
TO TELL WHETHER A FIGURE CAN BE TRACED AS DESCRIBED
ABOVE. IT IS EXPLAINED ON THE NEXT PAGE.

EULER LINES

EULER CLASSIFIED INTERSECTIONS OF LINES AS EVEN AND ODD VERTICES.

EVEN VERTICES   ODD VERTICES

HE NOTICED THAT THE NUMBER OF ODD VERTICES IN A FIGURE IS ALWAYS EVEN.

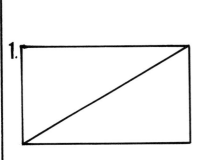

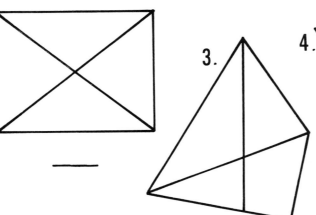

1.

2.

3.

4.

HOW MANY ODD VERTICES?

HERE'S SOME HELP ON THE PROBLEMS ON THE LAST PAGE.

1) IF A FIGURE HAS NO ODD VERTICES, YOU CAN TRACE IT STARTING AT ANY VERTEX.

2) IF A FIGURE HAS TWO ODD VERTICES, START AT ONE AND FINISH AT THE OTHER.

3) IF A FIGURE HAS OTHER THAN 0 OR 2 ODD VERTICES, IT IS NOT POSSIBLE TO TRACE IT WITHOUT CROSSING OR RETRACING ANOTHER LINE.

THE ILLUSTRATION SHOWN BELOW IS A COMPLETED GAME OF **HEX.**

HEX IS PLAYED BY TWO PLAYERS ON AN 11 X 11 FIELD OF **HEXAGONS.**

TO WIN AT HEX, A PLAYER MUST COMPLETE A CHAIN OF HIS MARKS FROM ONE SIDE OF THE BOARD TO THE OTHER SIDE.

THE FIRST PLAYER TO COMPLETE THE CHAIN ACROSS THE BOARD WINS.

BEFORE BEGINNING PLAY, PLAYERS MUST DECIDE WHICH PAIR OF OPPOSITE SIDES THEY ARE TRYING TO CONNECT.

ON YOUR TURN YOU CAN COVER ANY HEXAGON ON THE BOARD THAT HASN'T BEEN COVERED.

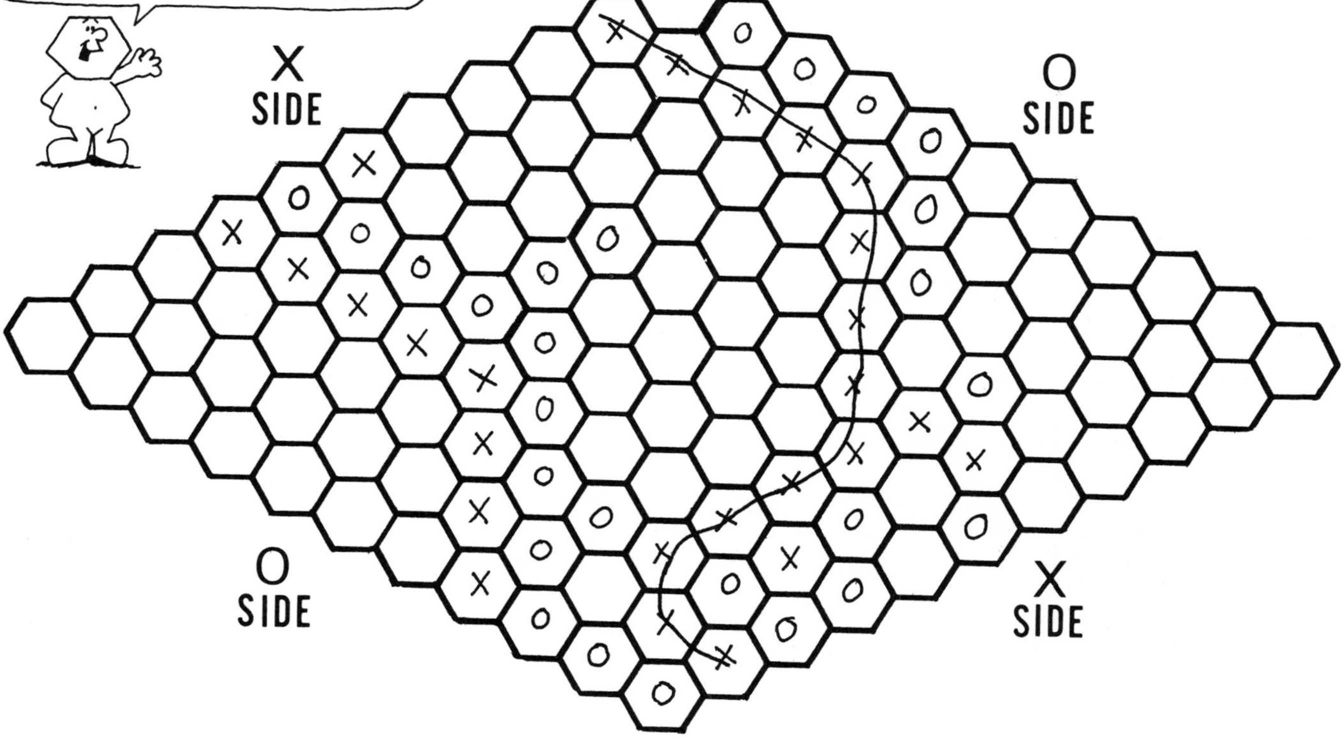

X SIDE

O SIDE

O SIDE

X SIDE

THIS HEXBOARD CAN BE MADE MORE PERMANENT IF IT IS GLUED ONTO A PIECE OF HEAVY TAGBOARD OR MASONITE.

IF YOU WANTED TO MAKE A LARGER HEXBOARD, COULD YOU MAKE PATTERNS LIKE THIS WITH A COMPASS AND RULER?

TRELLIS TWISTER

THE TRELLIS IN THE TOP LEFT-HAND CORNER IS
ONE OF THE OTHER EIGHT AS SEEN FROM THE
BACK SIDE. WHICH ONE?

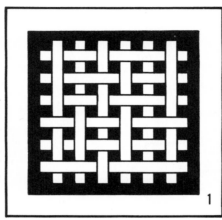

1

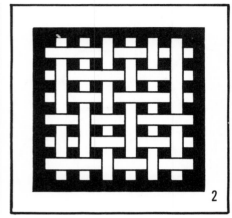

2

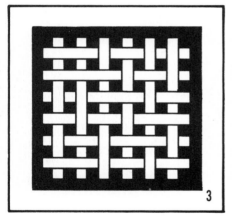

3

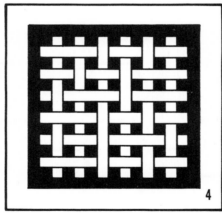

4

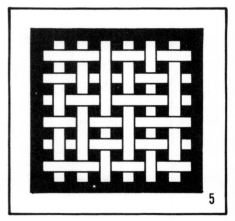

5

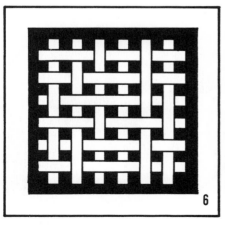

6

7

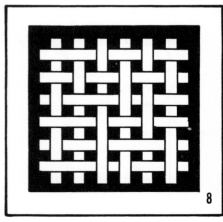

8

HIDDEN SHAPES

THE EIGHT SHADED FIGURES BELOW ARE ALL CREATED FROM THE
PATTERN IN THE CENTER. CAN YOU SEE HOW EACH PATTERN WAS
MADE? NOTICE HOW THE SHADING GIVES AN ILLUSION OF DEPTH.
PLACE A PIECE OF TRACING PAPER OVER THE CENTER PATTERN
AND CREATE SOME DESIGNS OF YOUR OWN.

WAY-OUT NUMERATION

HERE IS A NUMBER SYSTEM THAT I INVENTED WHEN I WAS NINE YEARS OLD.

BENJIE MAIDEN
NUEVA DAY SCHOOL

MY SYMBOLS ARE:

1	2	3	4	5	6	7	8	9
○	⬭	△	□	☆	✡	☆	☼	☀

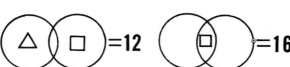

=12

LIKE 3 X 4

=16

LIKE 4 X 4

=11

12 – 1

=15

16 – 1

ANY NUMBER CAN BE WRITTEN IN THIS SYSTEM!

10 = ⬭ ☆

14 = ⬭ ☆

19 = □ ☆

13 = ⬭ △

17 = △ ✡

21 = △ ☆

(CONTINUED)

WAY-OUT NUMERATION

WHAT ARE THESE NUMERALS IN BENJIE'S SYSTEM?

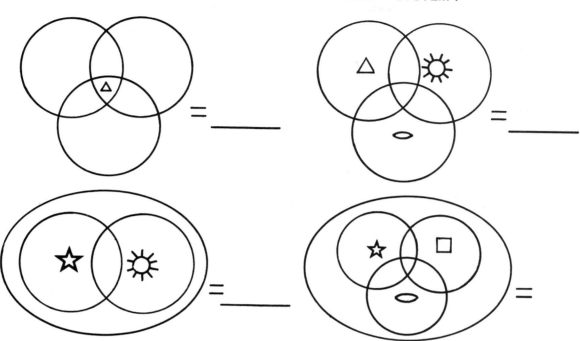

= _____

= _____

= _____

= _____

FILL IN THE SYMBOLS TO FORM THESE NUMBERS.

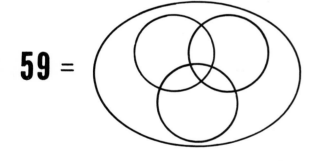

59 =

OR

72 =

OR

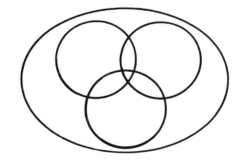

DRAW DIAGRAMS FOR BENJIE'S NUMERALS 30 THROUGH 40.

WHAT ARE SOME OF THE PROBLEMS WITH BENJIE'S SYSTEM?

QUADRILATERAL QUEST

A QUADRILATERAL IS A FOUR-SIDED POLYGON. CONNECT THE MIDPOINTS OF THE ADJACENT SIDES OF EACH OF THE QUADRILATERALS. WHAT KIND OF FIGURE DO YOU GET IN EACH CASE?

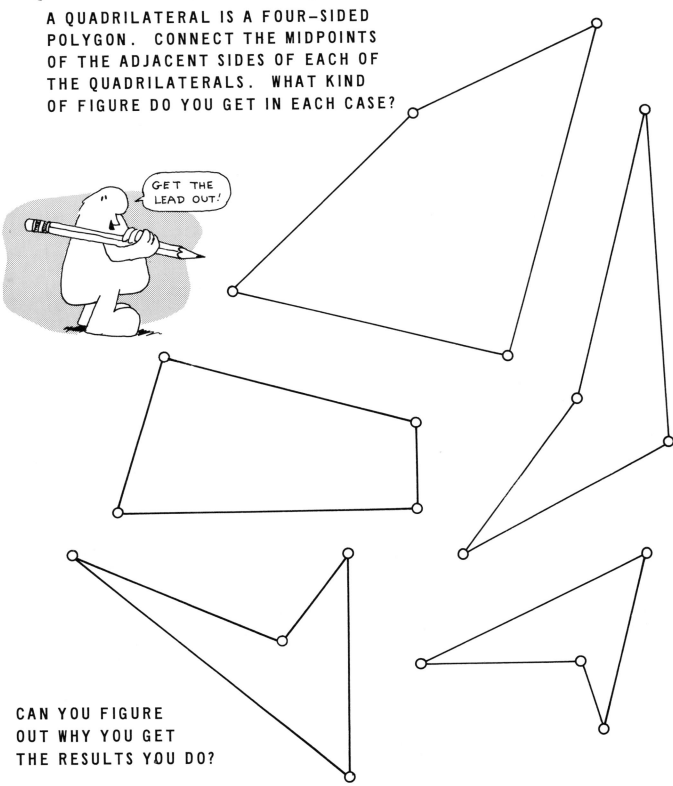

CAN YOU FIGURE OUT WHY YOU GET THE RESULTS YOU DO?

NUMBER PATTERNS

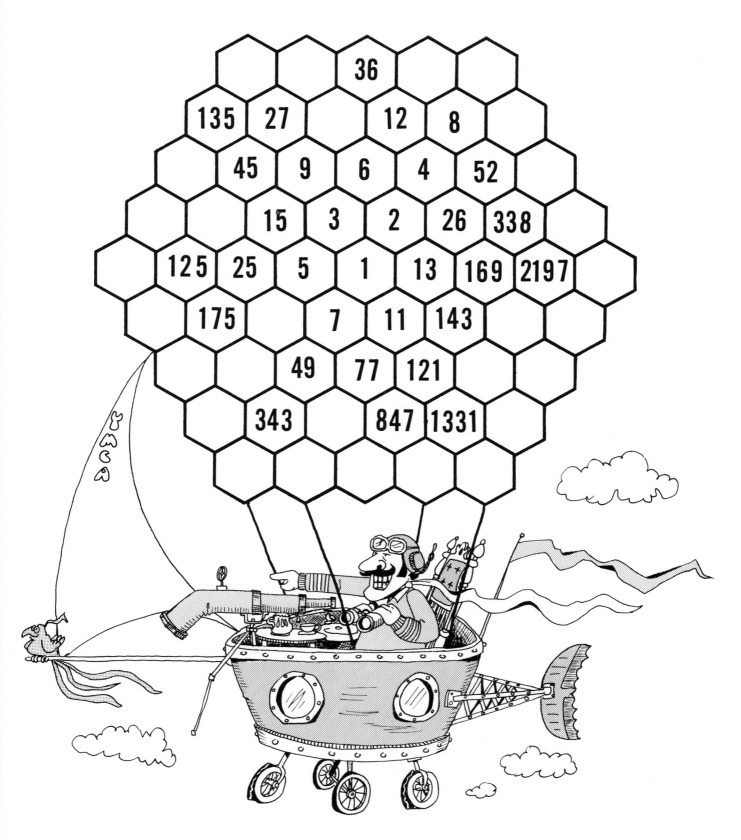

DECODE USING ALPHABET

TILE TRIAL

USE EACH OF THESE NUMBERS **ONCE** WITH ANY COMBINATION OF THE OPERATIONS X, +, −, ÷ TO MAKE A TRUE EQUATION.

15   **4**   **10**   **19**   **22**

EXAMPLE :

$\boxed{19} - \boxed{4} - \boxed{15} + \boxed{22} - \boxed{10} = 12$

1

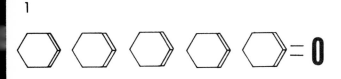 $= 0$

2

$\bigcirc\ \bigcirc\ \bigcirc\ \bigcirc\ \bigcirc = 1$

3

$\bigcirc\ \bigcirc\ \bigcirc\ \bigcirc\ \bigcirc = 2$

4

$\bigcirc\ \bigcirc\ \bigcirc\ \bigcirc\ \bigcirc = 3$

5

 $= 4$

6

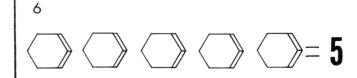 $= 5$

7

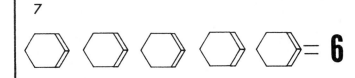 $= 6$

8

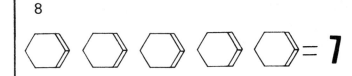 $= 7$

IT MAY BE EASIER TO WRITE THE FIVE NUMBERS ON SCRAPS OF PAPER SO THAT YOU CAN MOVE THEM AROUND.

ORDER SORTER

EACH TRIANGULAR REGION BELOW HAS A DIFFERENT AREA.

SEE IF YOU CAN ARRANGE THE LETTERS REPRESENTING THE REGIONS IN **ORDER** FROM THE SMALLEST TO THE LARGEST.

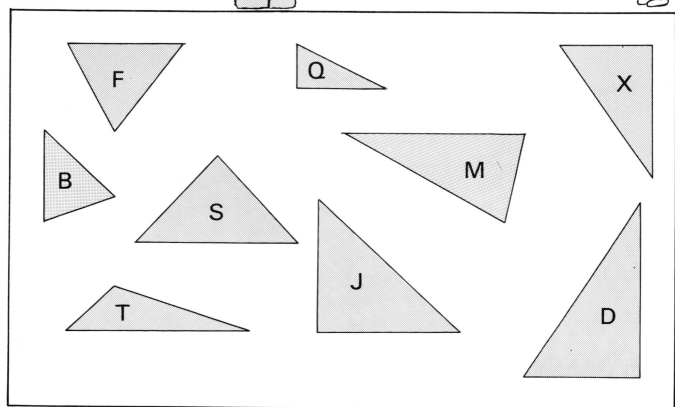

____ < ____ < ____ < ____ < ____ < ____ < ____ < ____ < ____

 SMALLEST

LARGEST

USE THIS CHART TO DECODE THE LETTERS IN YOUR ANSWER.

A	B	C	D	E	F	G	H	I	J	K	L	M	N	O	P	Q	R	S	T	U	V	W	X	Y	Z
F	R	U	S	K	A	P	C	Z	E	O	Y	L	X	H	W	T	Q	G	I	M	D	J	N	V	B

____ ____ ____ ____ ____ ____ ____ ____ ____

CREATIVE COLORING

WHICH ONE DIFFERS ?

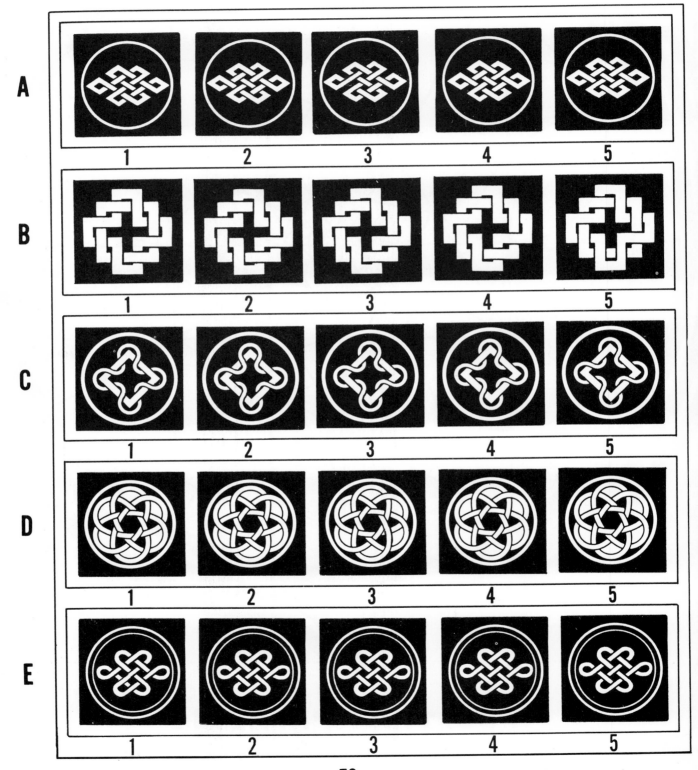

PLOTTING PICTURES

GRAPH THE FOLLOWING POINTS AND CONNECT EACH
POINT WITH THE NEXT POINT USING STRAIGHT LINE SEGMENTS.

CONNECT (−8,−9),(−4,−4),−4,2),(2,2),(4,4),(1,5),(−5,5),(−8,4) (−4,2).

CONNECT (2,2),(2,−4),(5,−9),(2,−14),(−5,−14),(−8,−9),(−11,−8),
(−8,−13) AND (−5,−14).

CONNECT (−11,−8),(−11,−2) AND (−8,4).

CONNECT (4,4),(8,−2),(8,−8),(5,−13) AND (2,−14).

CONNECT (8,−8) AND (5,−9).

CONNECT (2,−4) AND (−4,−4).

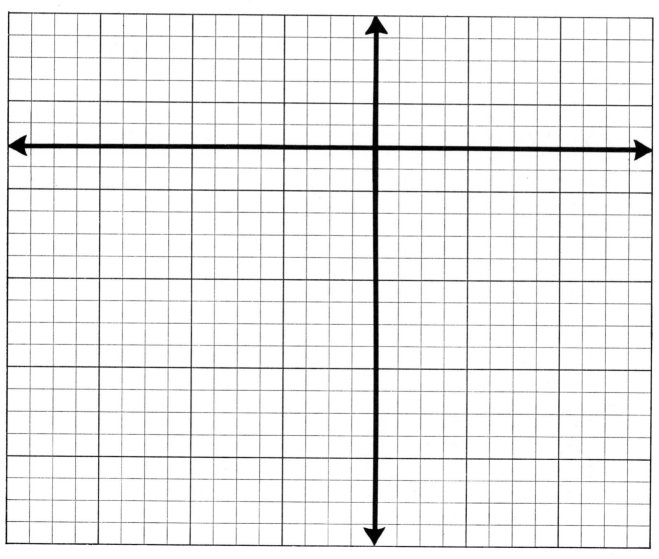

73

GEOMETRY IN BRIDGES

CAN YOU DESCRIBE THE GEOMETRY IN THE SHAPES OF THESE BRIDGES?

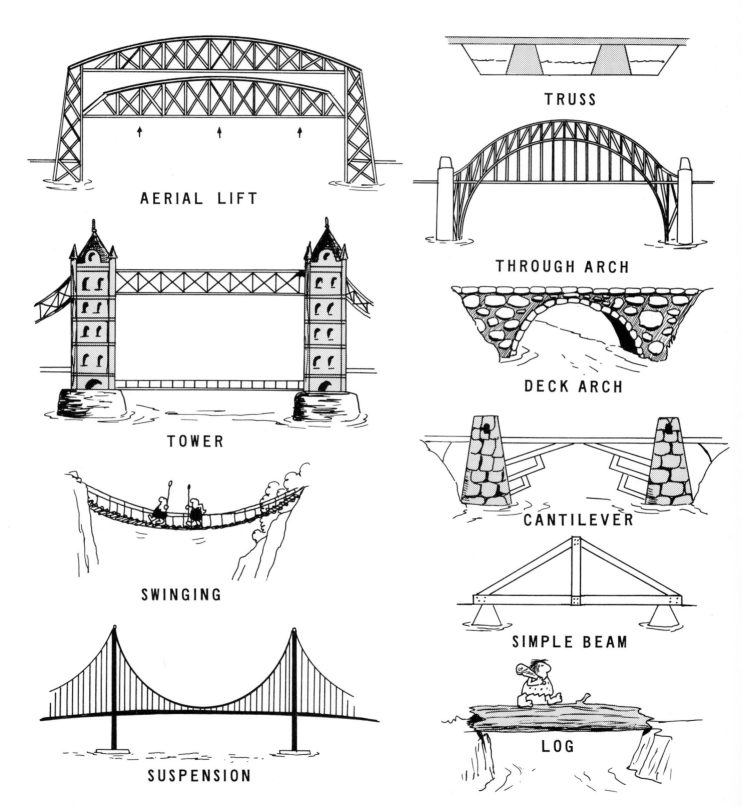

AERIAL LIFT

TRUSS

THROUGH ARCH

DECK ARCH

TOWER

CANTILEVER

SWINGING

SIMPLE BEAM

SUSPENSION

LOG

KNIGHT 'N DAZE

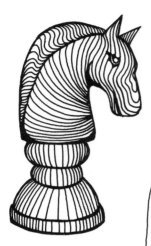

A KNIGHT IN CHESS MOVES TWO OVER AND ONE TO THE RIGHT OR LEFT.

IF I WERE IN THE CENTER, I COULD MOVE TO ANY OF THESE SQUARES.

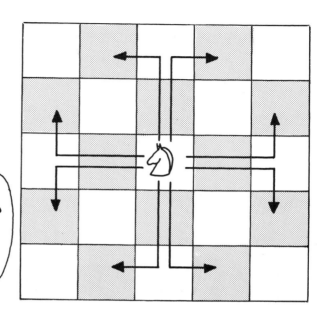

ON WHICH SQUARES COULD THE KNIGHT LAND?

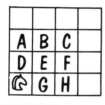

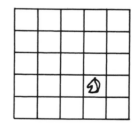

MARK IN THE SQUARES WHERE THE KNIGHT COULD MOVE.

IT IS POSSIBLE FOR THE KNIGHT TO MOVE IN EVERY SQUARE ON THIS 5 X 5 GRID WITHOUT LANDING IN THE SAME SQUARE TWICE. NUMBER THE MOVES — 1, 2, 3, 4, ... UP TO 25. **PLACE EVEN NUMBERS ON SHADED SQUARES.**

CONCENTRIC CIRCLES

CONCENTRIC CIRCLES ARE CIRCLES WHICH HAVE
THE SAME CENTER BUT DIFFERENT RADII.

WHICH FIGURES BELOW ILLUSTRATE CONCENTRIC CIRCLES ?

CUBE FLIP AND TURN

A CUBE CAN OCCUPY A SPACE IN 24 DIFFERENT WAYS.
CAN YOU FILL IN THE MISSING LETTERS?

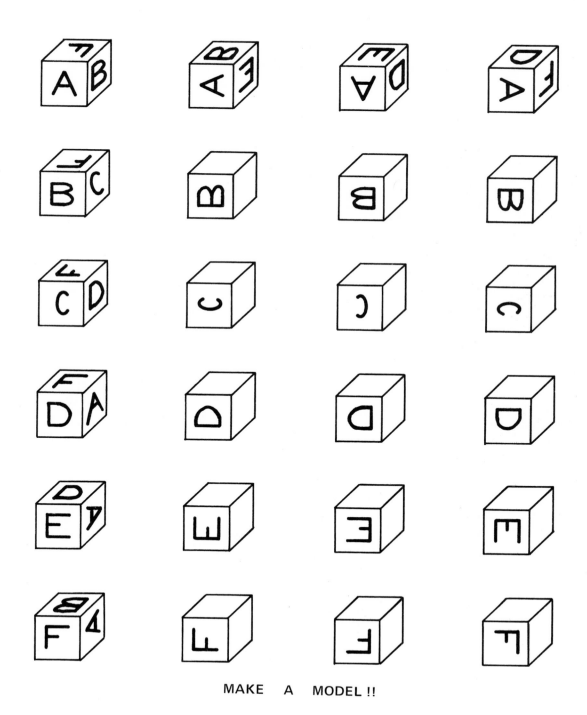

MAKE A MODEL !!

POLYOMINOES

THE 12 SHAPES BELOW ARE MADE WITH FIVE SQUARES. HOW MANY CAN YOU MAKE WITH SIX? WHICH ONE OF THE 12 FIGURES CAN BE DRAWN WITH SEVEN LINE SEGMENTS?
CUT OUT LARGE SHAPES LIKE THOSE BELOW AND FORM A 6X10 RECTANGLE. THE PUZZLE CAN BE DONE IN MORE THAN 2000 WAYS.

THE STORY IS TOLD THAT:

MANY YEARS AGO IN THE FAR OFF LAND OF CHANZANIA, A PRISONER WAS TO BE EXECUTED.

HELP!

THE KING OF CHANZANIA WAS A SPORTING FELLOW WHO THOUGHT HIGHLY OF GOOD THINKERS.

I THINK HIGHLY OF GOOD THINKERS.

THE KING OFFERED THE PRISONER A CHANCE FOR FREEDOM. HE WAS GIVEN 100 BLACK BALLS AND 100 WHITE BALLS, AND WAS TOLD TO DISTRIBUTE THEM INTO THREE SIMILAR URNS IN ANY WAY HE LIKED. HE WAS THEN BLINDFOLDED AND TOLD TO DRAW A BALL AT RANDOM FROM ONE OF THE URNS. IF HE DREW A BLACK BALL HE WOULD BE EXECUTED. IF HE DREW A WHITE BALL, HE WOULD HAVE HIS FREEDOM. (THE URNS WERE REARRANGED.)

I THINK HIGHLY OF GOOD THINKERS.

THE PRISONER WAS SMART (AND LUCKY), SO HE WAS SET FREE.

HOW WOULD YOU HAVE DISTRIBUTED THE BALLS IN THE THREE URNS?

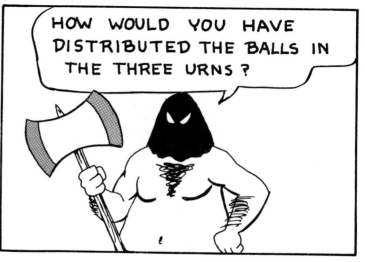

PUZZLERS

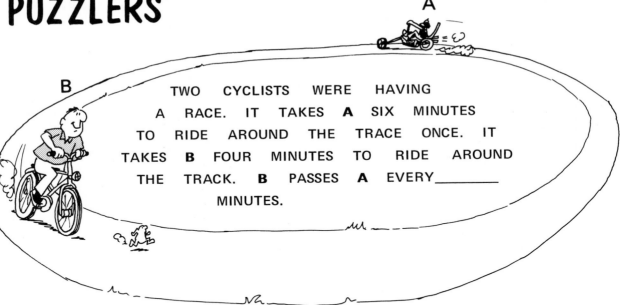

TWO CYCLISTS WERE HAVING A RACE. IT TAKES **A** SIX MINUTES TO RIDE AROUND THE TRACE ONCE. IT TAKES **B** FOUR MINUTES TO RIDE AROUND THE TRACK. **B** PASSES **A** EVERY_____ MINUTES.

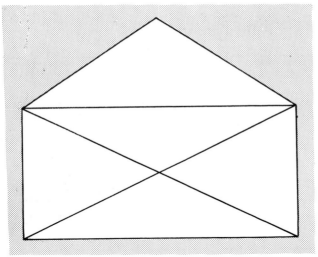

CAN YOU COPY THIS DRAWING OF AN ENVELOPE WITHOUT RAISING YOUR PEN OR PENCIL FROM THE PAPER? DON'T GO OVER ANY LINE TWICE !

ABOUT HOW LONG WOULD IT TAKE YOU TO COUNT TO ONE MILLION IF YOU COUNTED ONCE EVERY SECOND ?

ONE HUNDRED THOUSAND, FIFTY THREE, ONE HUNDRED THOUSAND, FIFTY FOUR, ONE ....

HOW MANY?

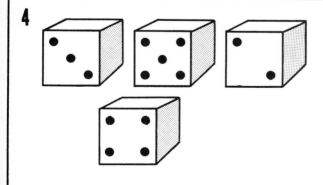

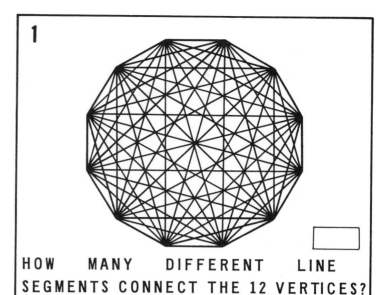

HOW MANY DIFFERENT LINE SEGMENTS CONNECT THE 12 VERTICES?

2

HOW MANY MULTIPLES OF 3? _____

3

HOW MANY SQUARES? _____

4

HOW MANY DIFFERENT NUMBER COMBINATIONS ON 4 DICE TOTAL 14?

THERE ARE EIGHT "HOW MANY" PAGES IN THE AFTERMATH SERIES. MANY OF THESE PROBLEMS LIKE 1 AND 3 HAVE PATTERNS TO THEIR SOLUTIONS. YOU MAY LIKE TO FIND A GENERAL RULE FOR SOME OF THESE PROBLEMS.

TINKERTOTALS

IN BOOKS ONE, TWO, AND THREE, YOU HAD A CHANCE TO TRY SOME TINKERTOTAL PUZZLES. HERE ARE SOME THAT ARE A LITTLE HARDER.

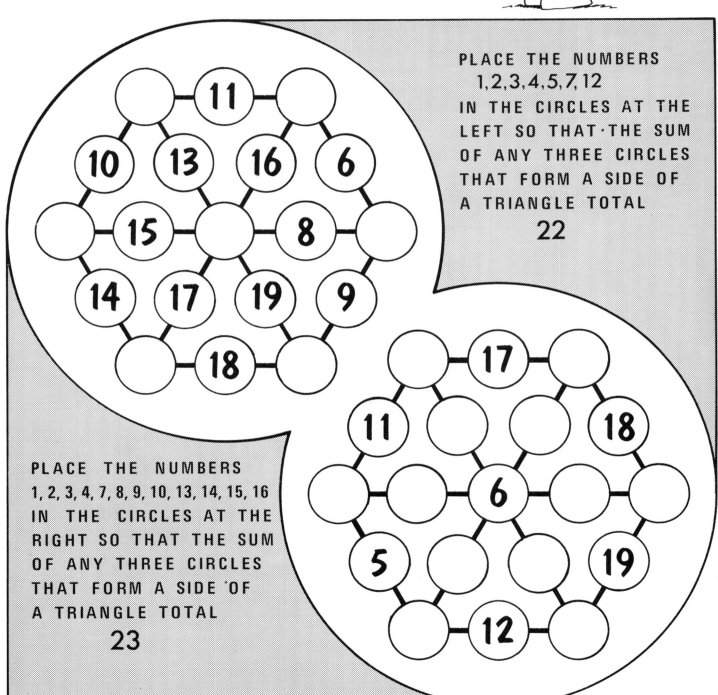

PLACE THE NUMBERS 1, 2, 3, 4, 5, 7, 12 IN THE CIRCLES AT THE LEFT SO THAT THE SUM OF ANY THREE CIRCLES THAT FORM A SIDE OF A TRIANGLE TOTAL **22**

PLACE THE NUMBERS 1, 2, 3, 4, 7, 8, 9, 10, 13, 14, 15, 16 IN THE CIRCLES AT THE RIGHT SO THAT THE SUM OF ANY THREE CIRCLES THAT FORM A SIDE OF A TRIANGLE TOTAL **23**

NAME GAME

CAN YOU FIND 100 MATH WORDS?

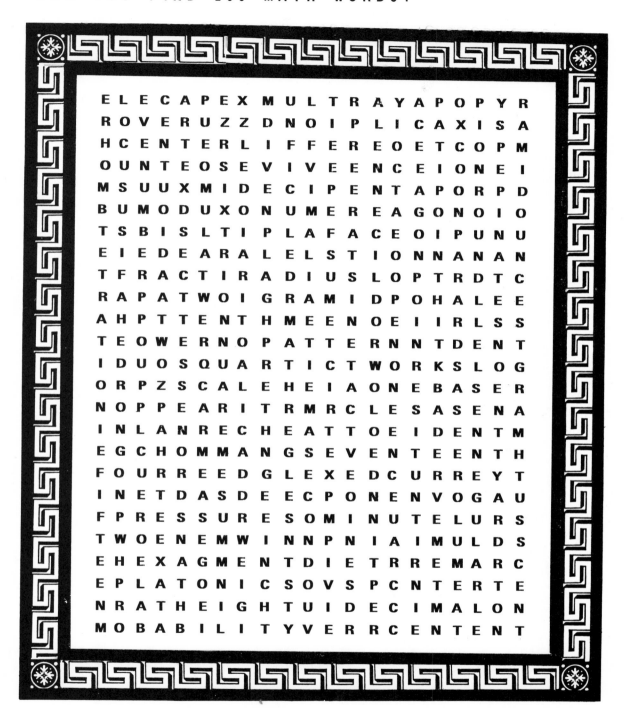

```
E L E C A P E X M U L T R A Y A P O P Y R
R O V E R U Z Z D N O I P L I C A X I S A
H C E N T E R L I F F E R E O E T C O P M
O U N T E O S E V I V E E N C E I O N E I
M S U U X M I D E C I P E N T A P O R P D
B U M O D U X O N U M E R E A G O N O I O
T S B I S L T I P L A F A C E O I P U N U
E I E D E A R A L E L S T I O N N A N A N
T F R A C T I R A D I U S L O P T R D T C
R A P A T W O I G R A M I D P O H A L E E
A H P T T E N T H M E E N O E I I R L S S
T E O W E R N O P A T T E R N N T D E N T
I D U O S Q U A R T I C T W O R K S L O G
O R P Z S C A L E H E I A O N E B A S E R
N O P P E A R I T R M R C L E S A S E N A
I N L A N R E C H E A T T O E I D E N T M
E G C H O M M A N G S E V E N T E E N T H
F O U R R E E D G L E X E D C U R R E Y T
I N E T D A S D E E C P O N E N V O G A U
F P R E S S U R E S O M I N U T E L U R S
T W O E N E M W I N N P N I A I M U L D S
E H E X A G M E N T D I E T R R E M A R C
E P L A T O N I C S O V S P C N T E R T E
N R A T H E I G H T U I D E C I M A L O N
M O B A B I L I T Y V E R R C E N T E N T
```

HORIZONTAL, VERTICAL, OR ZIG-ZAG

ONE, TWO, THREE, FOUR...

USE ANY COMBINATION OF
THESE SYMBOLS TO MAKE THE
SENTENCES BELOW TRUE.

+, −, X, ÷, ◯.

1) 1	2	3	4 = 0	7) 1	2	3	4 = 10
2) 1	2	3	4 = 1	8) 1	2	3	4 = 13
3) 1	2	3	4 = 2	9) 1	2	3	4 = 14
4) 1	2	3	4 = 4	10) 1	2	3	4 = 20
5) 1	2	3	4 = 5	11) 1	2	3	4 = 21
6) 1	2	3	4 = 6	12) 1	2	3	4 = 24

FIND MY PATTERN

EACH OF THE NINE SMALL TRIANGLES AT THE RIGHT REPRESENT ONE OF THE DIGITS: 1, 2, 3, 4, 5, 6, 7, 8, 9.

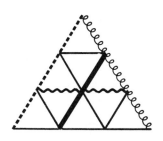

USING NUMBER PROPERTIES AND PATTERNS IN THE SENTENCES AT THE LEFT.. CAN YOU IDENTIFY EACH OF THE NINE SYMBOLS?

I CAN TRI.

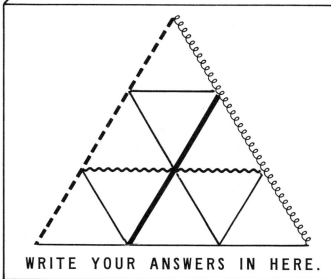

WRITE YOUR ANSWERS IN HERE.

85

PROPORTIONAL DRAWING

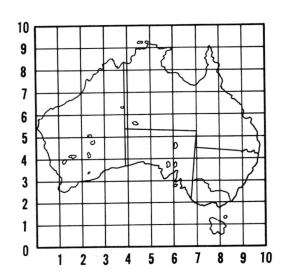

MAKE AN ENLARGEMENT OF THE DRAWING AT THE LEFT ON THE GRID BELOW.

A LINE ON THE SMALL GRID SHOULD BE LOCATED ON A CORRESPONDING POSITION ON THE LARGE GRID.

THE AREA OF THE TWO DRAWINGS ARE IN THE RATIO OF 4 TO 1.

IF YOU DOUBLE THE DIMENSIONS YOU GET FOUR TIMES THE AREA.

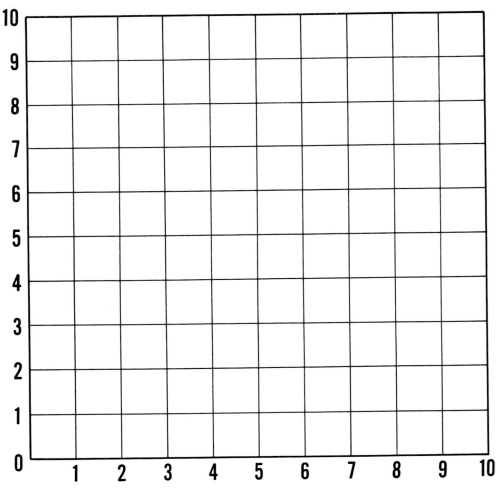

DIJAKNOWTHAT

UNTIL JULY 1951, THE LARGEST KNOWN PRIME NUMBER WAS:

$$2^{127} - 1 = 170, 141, 183, 460, 469, 231, 731, 687,$$
$$303, 715, 884, 105, 727.$$

NOW WITH THE USE OF COMPUTERS, SEVERAL LARGER PRIME NUMBERS HAVE BEEN DISCOVERED.

THE NUMBER OF PRIMES IS INFINITE?

HOW MANY IS THAT?

EVERY EVEN NUMBER GREATER THAN TWO CAN BE WRITTEN AS THE SUM OF TWO PRIMES? TRY IT!

12345679 · 9	=	111111111
12345679 · 18	=	222222222
12345679 · 27	=	333333333
12345679 · 36	=	444444444
12345679 · 45	=	555555555
12345679 · 54	=	666666666
12345679 · 63	=	777777777
12345679 · __	=	888888888
12345679 · __	=	_____

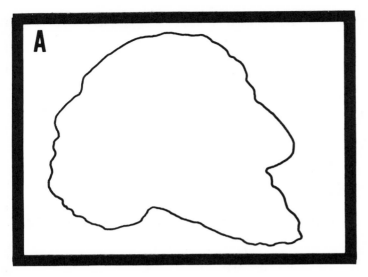

COLORING MATH MAPS

AN OUTLINE OF THE ISLAND OF RUM IS SHOWN AT THE LEFT. THE SURROUNDING WATER IS AL-WAYS COLORED BLUE. WITH THE DIVISIONS AS DRAWN, WHAT IS THE FEWEST POSSIBLE NUMBER OF COLORS NEEDED TO "PROPERLY COLOR" EACH?

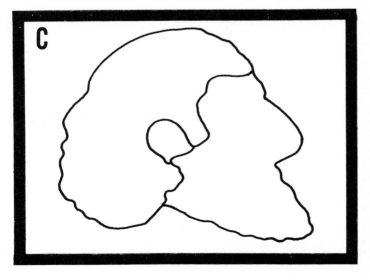

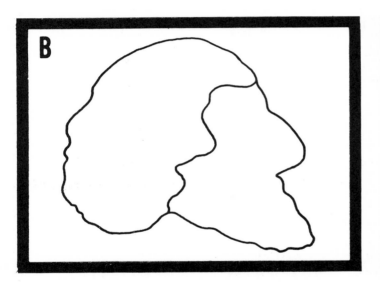

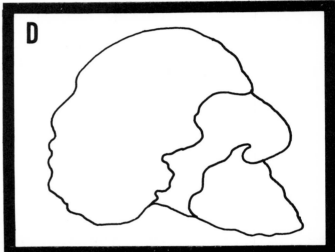

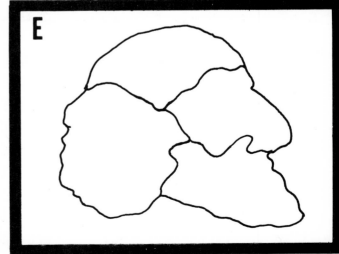

COLORING MATH MAPS

COMPLETE THIS CHART USING THIS PAGE AND THE PREVIOUS PAGE.

FIGURE	REGIONS	COLORS NEEDED
A	2	2
B	3	
C		
D		
E		
F		
G		
H		
I		
J		

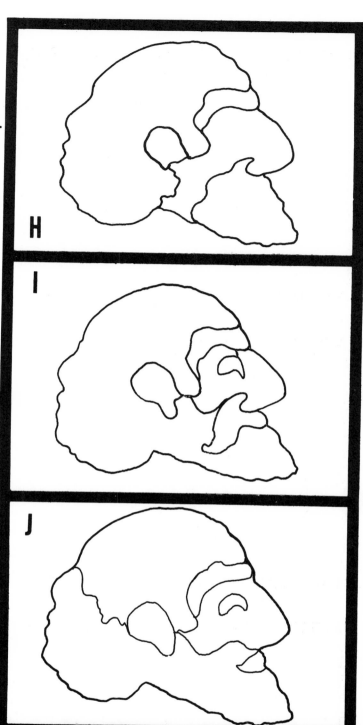

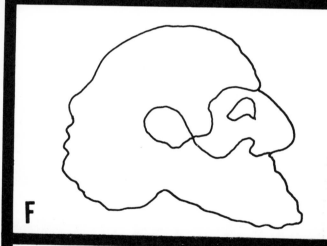

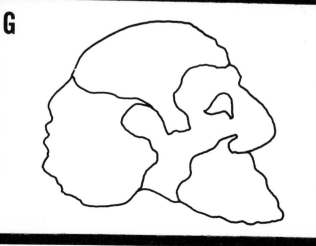

IT HAS BEEN PROVEN THAT FIVE COLORS ARE SUFFICIENT TO COLOR ANY MAP, BUT NO MAP HAS EVER BEEN CREATED FOR WHICH FIVE COLORS ARE NECESSARY.

DIJAKNOWTHAT

PRIMES THAT DIFFER BY TWO ARE CALLED TWIN PRIMES? (THERE ARE 16 TWIN PRIMES AMONG THE FIRST 100 NUMBERS).

CAN YOU LIST THESE 16?

HOW ABOUT TRIPLETS?

$1^3 = 1$
$2^3 = 3 + 5$
$3^3 = 7 + 9 + 11$
$4^3 = 13 + 15 + 17 + 19$
$5^3 = ?$
$6^3 = ?$

$$1^3 + 5^3 + 3^3 = 153$$
$$4^3 + 0^3 + 7^3 = 407$$
$$3^3 + 4^3 + 5^3 = 6^3$$
$$(20+25)^2 = 2025$$
$$(30+25)^2 = 3025$$
$$(40+25)^2 = ?$$

WATERS THE MATTER WITH YOU?

HELP!

PATTERNS AND SEQUENCES

FIND THE PATTERN AND FILL IN THE MISSING NUMBERS.

1 6 · 12 · 18 · 24 · ☐ · ☐ · ☐

2 3 · 9 · 27 · 81 · ☐ · ☐ · ☐

3 $\frac{1}{2}$ · $\frac{1}{4}$ · $\frac{1}{8}$ · ☐ · ☐ · ☐ · ☐

4 .125 · .25 · .375 · .5 · ☐ · ☐ · ☐

5 6 · 4 · 2 · 0 · −2 · ☐ · ☐

6 .1 · .1 · .2 · .3 · .5 · ☐ · ☐

7 1 · 1·2 · 1·2·3 · 24 · ☐ · ☐ · ☐

8 1_5 · 4_5 · 12_5 · 20_5 · ☐ · ☐ · ☐

9 1_7 · 4_7 · 12_7 · 22_7 · ☐ · ☐ · ☐

91

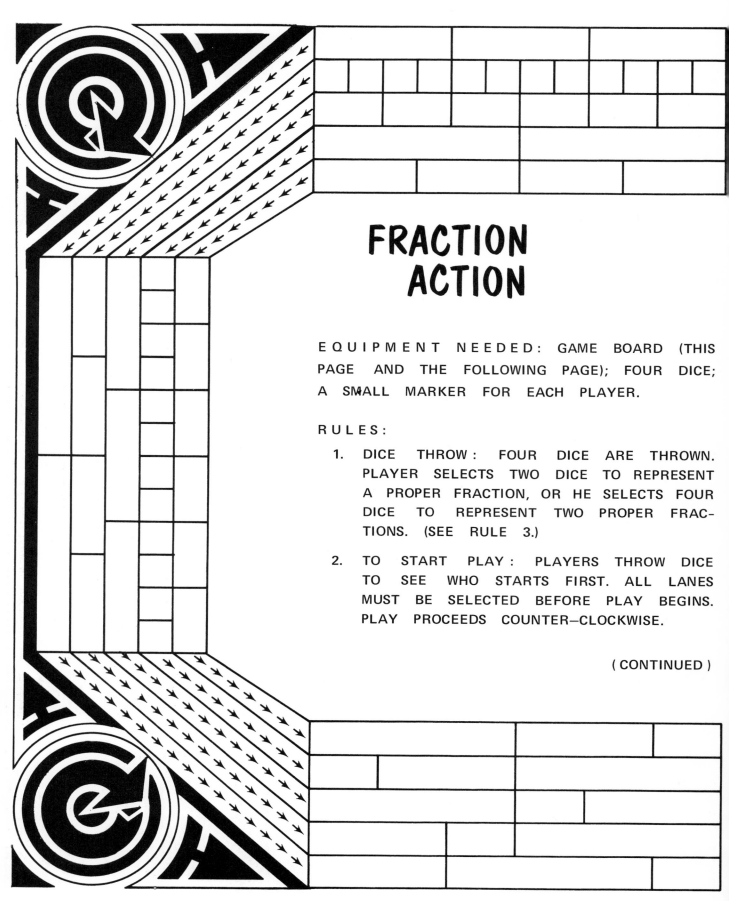

FRACTION ACTION

EQUIPMENT NEEDED: GAME BOARD (THIS PAGE AND THE FOLLOWING PAGE); FOUR DICE; A SMALL MARKER FOR EACH PLAYER.

RULES:

1. DICE THROW: FOUR DICE ARE THROWN. PLAYER SELECTS TWO DICE TO REPRESENT A PROPER FRACTION, OR HE SELECTS FOUR DICE TO REPRESENT TWO PROPER FRACTIONS. (SEE RULE 3.)

2. TO START PLAY: PLAYERS THROW DICE TO SEE WHO STARTS FIRST. ALL LANES MUST BE SELECTED BEFORE PLAY BEGINS. PLAY PROCEEDS COUNTER–CLOCKWISE.

(CONTINUED)

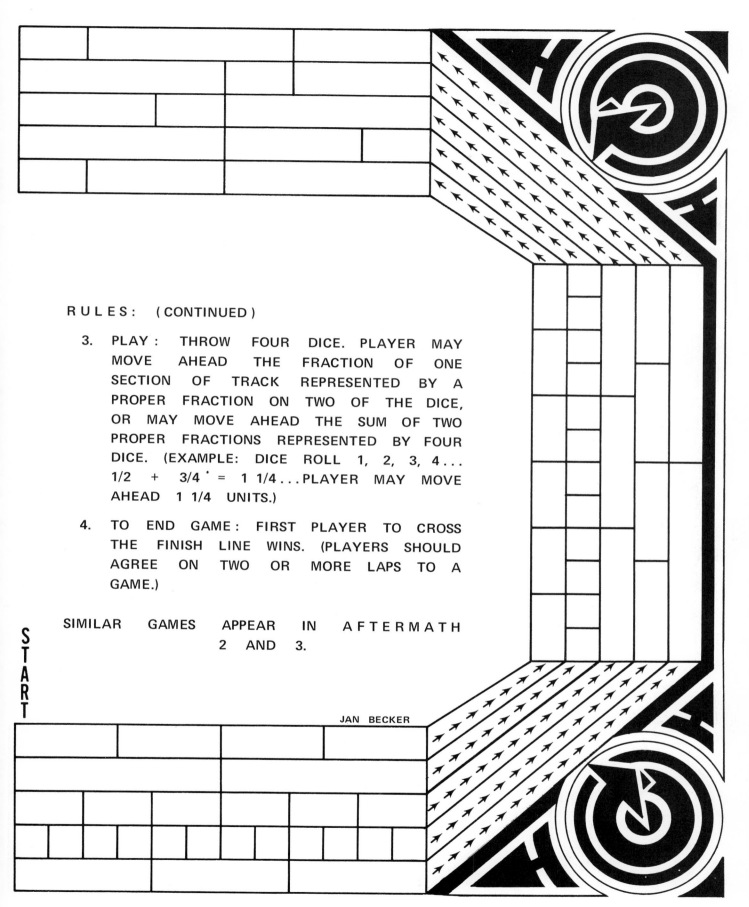

RULES: (CONTINUED)

3. PLAY: THROW FOUR DICE. PLAYER MAY MOVE AHEAD THE FRACTION OF ONE SECTION OF TRACK REPRESENTED BY A PROPER FRACTION ON TWO OF THE DICE, OR MAY MOVE AHEAD THE SUM OF TWO PROPER FRACTIONS REPRESENTED BY FOUR DICE. (EXAMPLE: DICE ROLL 1, 2, 3, 4... $1/2 + 3/4 = 1 1/4$...PLAYER MAY MOVE AHEAD 1 1/4 UNITS.)

4. TO END GAME: FIRST PLAYER TO CROSS THE FINISH LINE WINS. (PLAYERS SHOULD AGREE ON TWO OR MORE LAPS TO A GAME.)

SIMILAR GAMES APPEAR IN AFTERMATH 2 AND 3.

START

JAN BECKER

POWER PATTERNS

$1 =$

$1^3 =$

$1 + 2 =$

$1^3 + 2^3 =$

$1 + 2 + 3 =$

$1^3 + 2^3 + 3^3 =$

$1 + 2 + 3 + 4 =$

$1^3 + 2^3 + 3^3 + 4^3 =$

$1 + 2 + 3 + 4 + 5 =$

$1^3 + 2^3 + 3^3 + 4^3 + 5^3 =$

$1 + 2 + 3 + 4 + 5 + 6 =$

$1^3 + 2^3 + 3^3 + 4^3 + 5^3 + 6^3 =$

$1 + 2 + 3 + \ldots + (n-1) + n = \dfrac{n(n+1)}{2}$

$1^3 + 2^3 + 3^3 + \ldots (n-1)^3 + n^3 = \left[\dfrac{n(n+1)}{2}\right]^2$

FIT THE DISCS

A C R O S S

A N D

D O W N

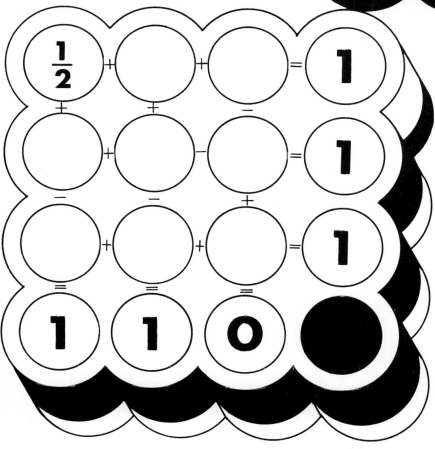

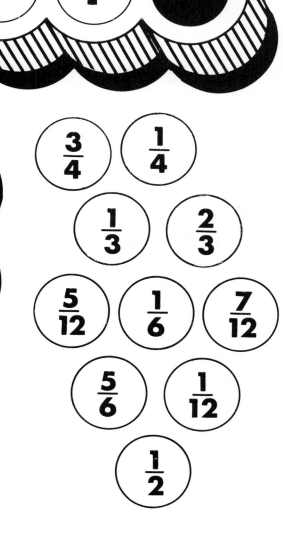

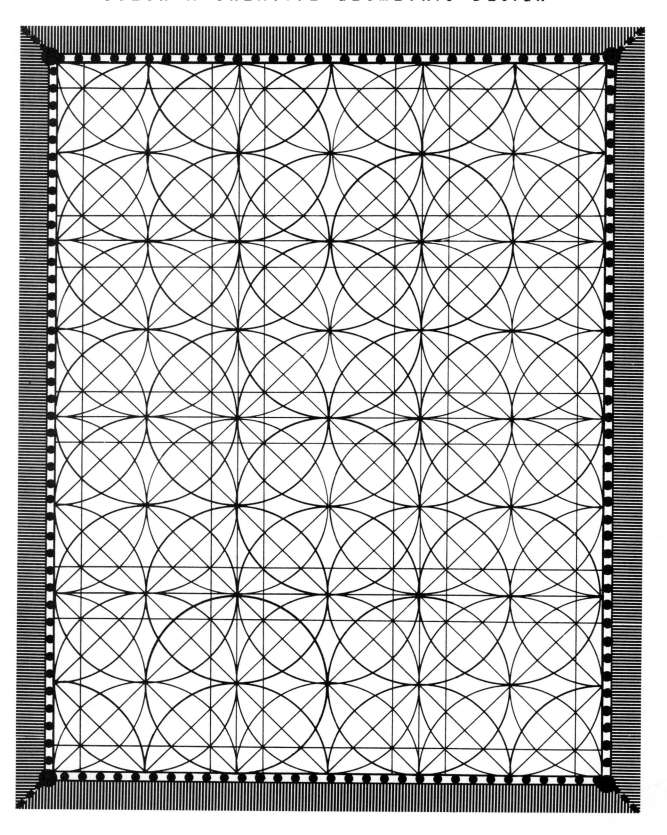

MAGIC HEXAGON

THE PUZZLE BELOW WAS CREATED BY 19 YEAR-OLD CLIFFORD ADAMS IN 1910. THE PUZZLE IS TO WRITE THE FIRST 19 POSITIVE INTEGERS IN THE 19 BLANK CELLS SO THAT ANY STRAIGHT LINE WILL ADD TO 38. IT IS A VERY DIFFICULT PUZZLE, SO WE HAVE HELPED A LITTLE BY FURNISHING SOME NUMBERS. TRY YOUR LUCK (AND LOGIC).

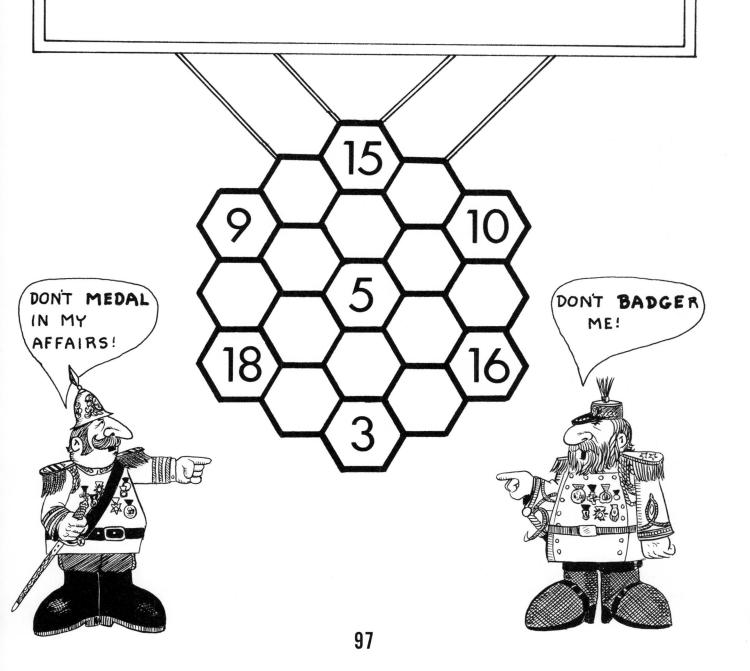

DON'T MEDAL IN MY AFFAIRS!

DON'T **BADGER** ME!

ACCURACY

THE SYMBOL ! TO THE RIGHT OF A NUMBER IS READ "FACTORIAL." THAT MEANS, MULTIPLY THE COUNTING NUMBERS UP TO AND INCLUDING THE NUMBER BESIDE THE ! .

$$1! = 1$$
$$2! = 1 \times 2 = 2$$
$$3! = 1 \times 2 \times 3 = 6$$
$$4! = 1 \times 2 \times 3 \times 4 = 24$$

THREE FACTORIAL (3!) GIVES THE NUMBER OF DIFFERENT WAYS THREE OBJECTS CAN BE ARRANGED.

$$3! = 3 \times 2 \times 1 = 6$$

$$\underbrace{\text{ABC} \quad \text{ACB} \quad \text{BAC} \quad \text{BCA} \quad \text{CAB} \quad \text{CBA}}_{6}$$

TO TEST YOUR ACCURACY IN COMPUTATION AND SEE HOW MANY DIFFERENT WAYS 14 OBJECTS CAN BE ARRANGED . . .

FIND 14! OR 14 x 13 x 12 x 11 x 10 x 9 x 8 x 6 x 6 x 5 x 4 x 3 x 2 x 1

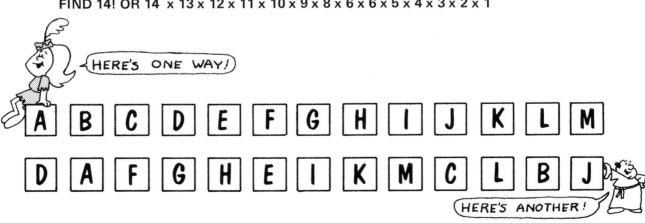

HERE'S ONE WAY!

| A | B | C | D | E | F | G | H | I | J | K | L | M |

| D | A | F | G | H | E | I | K | M | C | L | B | J |

HERE'S ANOTHER !

HIDDEN PRODUCTS

20	2	3	3	8	1	8	9	8	0	4	3	8	2	1	4
19	4	7	1	4	5	4	7	4	1	2	3	8	5	2	3
18	2	1	5	2	5	4	3	2	1	2	6	4	0	4	2
17	6	3	8	2	5	7	1	3	1	3	8	2	2	8	6
16	8	5	3	2	6	8	8	2	4	6	8	7	3	2	2
15	8	7	0	4	5	6	7	3	5	9	8	5	6	8	4
14	6	6	3	4	2	5	6	9	5	4	5	8	5	6	9
13	4	2	3	8	7	6	5	7	4	4	3	9	2	8	9
12	4	1	2	9	4	3	8	1	3	6	6	0	4	8	1
11	0	3	3	6	5	0	3	7	4	1	5	7	7	6	2
10	4	3	6	5	4	7	6	7	3	3	0	8	1	1	1
9	3	6	3	0	4	2	5	6	6	6	5	6	7	6	3
8	5	1	8	5	8	9	6	2	9	9	0	7	6	1	6
7	5	3	4	0	1	5	0	2	5	4	5	8	3	7	2
6	0	7	2	2	2	5	6	7	2	6	2	2	8	3	2
5	1	7	4	2	4	0	0	1	9	6	0	8	1	2	4
4	4	9	2	8	8	5	6	4	8	6	3	0	8	8	7
3	6	3	4	4	4	2	7	2	3	6	4	8	1	4	4
2	0	7	4	2	8	1	3	6	8	1	2	9	7	2	8
1	8	1	8	8	4	2	1	2	4	1	6	1	8	8	2
	1	2	3	4	5	6	7	8	9	10	11	12	13	14	15

IN THE ARRAY ABOVE, THERE ARE 57 HIDDEN MULTIPLICATION PROBLEMS. THE SOLUTIONS, INCLUDING PARTIAL PRODUCTS, ARE COMPLETE AND CORRECT. THERE ARE 46 PROBLEMS WITH ONE-DIGIT FACTORS; 10 WITH TWO-DIGIT FACTORS, AND ONE WITH THREE-DIGIT FACTORS. HOW MANY CAN YOU FIND?

DESCRIBE THE LOCATION OF EACH PROBLEM USING THE COORDINATES OF THE LEADING DIGIT OF THE NUMBER BEING MULTIPLIED.

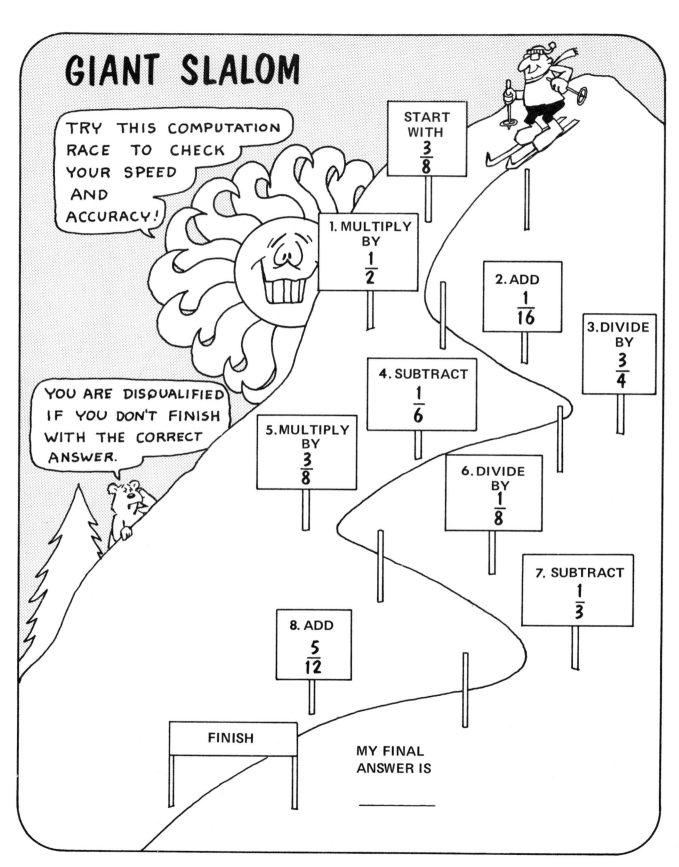

DIGIT DISCOVERY

FIVE GIRLS

FIVE GIRLS STOPPED IN FOR A SODA ON THE WAY HOME FROM SCHOOL.

THE GIRLS WERE AMAZED TO FIND THAT EACH OF THEM HAD EXACTLY **6** COINS.

EACH OF THEM HAD AT LEAST ONE EACH OF 4 TYPES OF COINS (PENNY, NICKEL, DIME AND QUARTER).

1. BETTY HAD ONE MORE NICKEL THAN ALICE, BUT ALICE HAD 5 CENTS MORE THAN BETTY ALTOGETHER.
2. DONNA HAD ONE MORE NICKEL THAN BETTY, BUT BETTY HAD 5 CENTS MORE THAN DONNA ALTOGETHER.
3. EVE HAD ONE MORE NICKEL THAN CAROL, BUT CAROL HAD 5 CENTS MORE THAN EVE ALTOGETHER.
4. CAROL HAD ONE MORE PENNY THAN DONNA AND SHE ALSO HAD 1 CENT MORE THAN DONNA ALTOGETHER.
5. **NONE OF THE GIRLS** HAD THE SAME AMOUNT OF MONEY.

HOW MUCH DID EACH GIRL HAVE?

HINT: MAKE A CHART OF THE POSSIBLE COMBINATIONS.

PHOTO ALBUM PAGES

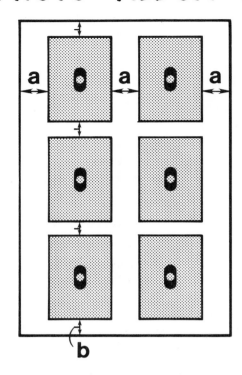

1. Album page: 11″ x 17″

O: $3\frac{1}{4}$″ x $4\frac{1}{2}$″

Find: a = _____ ″, b = _____ ″

2. Album page: 29 cm x 43 cm

P: 7.6 cm wide x 8.7 cm high

Q: 8.8 cm x 7.6 cm

Find: c = _____ cm, d = _____ cm,

e = _____ cm

3. Album page: 274 mm x 393 mm

R: 78 mm x 91 mm

S: 122 mm x 105 mm

Find: f = _____ mm, g = _____ mm,

h = _____ mm

IT MAY BE HELPFUL TO MAKE A MODEL OF THESE ALBUM PAGES.

104

PHOTO ALBUM PAGES

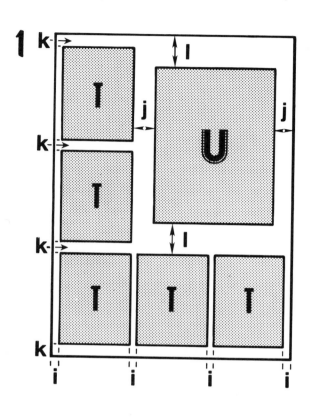

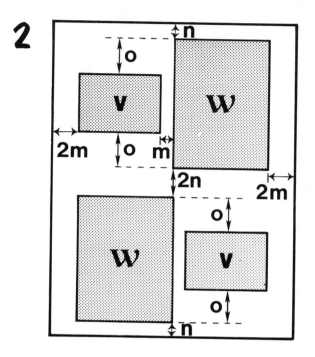

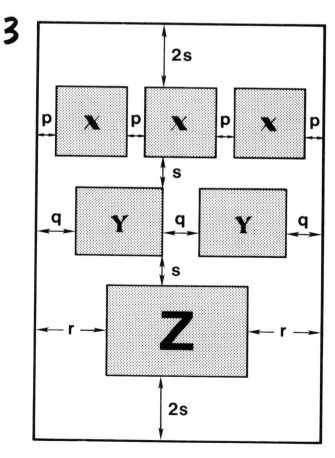

1. Album page: 26.2 cm x 35.8 cm

   T: 7.4 cm x 10.2 cm

   U: 12.8 cm x 17.7 cm

   Find: i = _____ cm, j = _____ cm,

         k = _____ cm, l = _____ cm

2. Album page: $13\frac{1}{2}$'' x 18''

   V: $4\frac{1}{2}$'' x $3\frac{1}{4}$''

   W: $5\frac{1}{4}$'' x $7\frac{1}{4}$''

   Find: m = _____'', n = _____'',

         o = _____''

3. Album page: 38.4 cm x 58.3 cm

   X: 9.6 cm x 9.6 cm

   Y: 11.4 cm x 9.2 cm

   Z: 19.0 cm x 12.5 cm

   Find: p = _____ cm, q = _____ cm,

         r = _____ cm, s = _____ cm

105

SOLUTIONS

BOOK FOUR

FRIDAY IN FRANCE, Pages 1–3

CAR NO.	CAR COLOR OR DECORATION	HELMET COLOR OR DECORATION	FINISH IN THE RACE
1	Polka Dot	Grey	4
2	Check	Stripe	1
3	Grey	Black	5
4	Black	Check	2
5	Stripe	Polka Dot	3

LETTER AREA, Page 4

A) 101
B) 120
C) 32
D) 38
E) 31
F) 28
G) 41

H) 43
I) 10
J) 24
K) 31 1/2
L) 21
M) 48

AREA AND PERIMETERS, Page 5

m (A) = 7 1/2"   m (E) = 9 3/4"
m (B) = 7 5/8"   m (F) = 12 1/2"
m (C) = 8 3/16"   m (G) = 19 1/2"
m (D) = 8 1/2"   TRUE

Your answers should not vary from these more than $\frac{1}{8}$" but remember, all measurement is approximate.

COIN CAPERS, Page 6

COIN CAPERS, Page 6 (cont.)

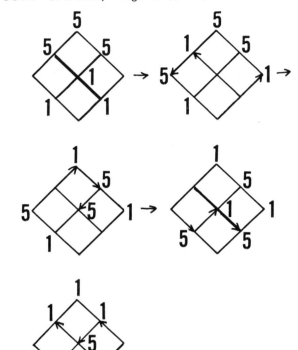

MOVING MATCHES, Page 7

I.

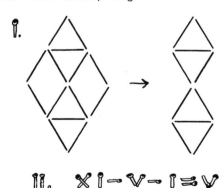

II.

III.

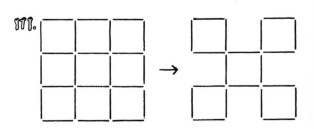

MAGIC SQUARE, Page 8

8	1	6
3	5	7
4	9	2

MATH PUN FUN, Page 9

YARD   POINT
BASE   CIRCLE
SEVEN   MATHEMATICS
NUMBER

        BLONDES

TILE TRIAL, Page 10

1) $10 \div (4 + 1) + 12 - 13 = 1$
2) $10 \div (4 + 1) \times (13 - 12) = 2$
3) $(13 - 12 + 10 + 1) \div 4 = 3$
4) $(13 + 12 - 10 + 1) \div 4 = 4$
5) $12 \div 4 + 13 - 10 - 1 = 5$
6) $12 \div (4 \times 1) + 13 - 10 = 6$
7) $(13 + 12 + 10) \div (1 + 4) = 7$
8) $13 - 12 + 10 + 1 - 4 = 8$

Answers are not unique.

STAR SEARCH, Page 11

1) 5   5) 10
2) 17   6) 2
3) 9   7) 5
4) 3   8) 0

PROFILE PUZZLE, Page 13

1) K   4) H   7) D   10) B
2) G   5) F   8) J   11) L
3) C   6) A   9) E   12) I

FAMOUS MATHEMATICIAN, Pages 14—15

        ARCHIMEDES

WANTED, Page 16

1) 4   5) 3
2) 6   6) 2
3) 5   7) 8
4) 1   8) 7

QUILT QUIZ, Page 17

PRIME PATTERN, Page 24

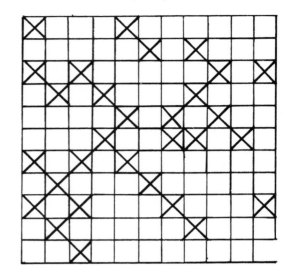

RATIO, Page 25

1) 4/8	5) 8/7	9) 8/10
2) 3/7	6) 7/4	10) 10/8
3) 3/4	7) 4/10	
4) 12/10	8) 12/7	

I'M A NUMBER GAME, Pages 18—19

A) 13 or 31   D) 256
B) 3/11   E) 624
C) 315   F) 147

A WHOLE THING, Page 27

1a) 1/6   2a) 1/5   3a) 3/14
1b) 1 1/2 2b) 19/20 3b) 14 sqs
1c) 2/3   2c) 1/20   3c) 4. sqs

BASE FOURTEEN, Page 28

$FOUR_{14}$ = 2 (2744) + 7 (196) + 11 (14) + 8 = 7022

SIX_{14} = 9 (196) + 5 (14) + 0 = 1834

$EIGHT_{14}$ = 1 (38416) + 5 (2744) + **3** (196) + 4 (14) + 10 = 52790

SUM DECIMALS, Page 21

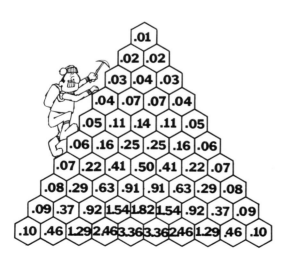

A WHOLE THING, Page 29

area of CDKL = $\frac{1}{3}$　　　area of DFHK = $\frac{5}{6}$
area of CDK = $\frac{1}{6}$　　　area of CFHK = 1
area of BGHM = $1\frac{2}{3}$　　area of EFHJ = $\frac{1}{2}$
area of CEJL = $\frac{2}{3}$

DOMINOE FACTORY MAZE, Page 30

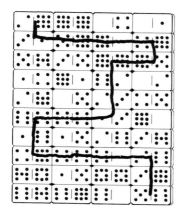

INTEGERS, Pages 34—35

+	-6	-5	-4	-3	-2	-1	0	1	2	3	4	5	6
-6	-12	-11	-10	-9	-8	-7	-6	-5	-4	-3	-2	-1	0
-5	-11	-10	-9	-8	-7	-6	-5	-4	-3	-2	-1	0	1
-4	-10	-9	-8	-7	-6	-5	-4	-3	-2	-1	0	1	2
-3	-9	-8	-7	-6	-5	-4	-3	-2	-1	0	1	2	3
-2	-8	-7	-6	-5	-4	-3	-2	-1	0	1	2	3	4
-1	-7	-6	-5	-4	-3	-2	-1	0	1	2	3	4	5
0	-6	-5	-4	-3	-2	-1	0	1	2	3	4	5	6
1	-5	-4	-3	-2	-1	0	1	2	3	4	5	6	7
2	-4	-3	-2	-1	0	1	2	3	4	5	6	7	8
3	-3	-2	-1	0	1	2	3	4	5	6	7	8	9
4	-2	-1	0	1	2	3	4	5	6	7	8	9	10
5	-1	0	1	2	3	4	5	6	7	8	9	10	11
6	0	1	2	3	4	5	6	7	8	9	10	11	12

INTEGERS, Pages 34—35 (cont.)

1) P + P = P
2) 3 + 5 = 8
3) P + N = P or N or 0
4) -3 + 5 = 2
5) -9 + 4 = -5
6) -6 + 6 = 0
7) N + N = N
8) -7 + (-5) = -12

1) P × P = P
2) 5 × 6 = 30
3) P × N = N
4) +5 × -6 = -30
5) 3 × (-4) = -12
6) N × N = P
7) -4 × -5 = 20

×	-6	-5	-4	-3	-2	-1	0	1	2	3	4	5	6
-6	36	30	24	18	12	6	0	-6	-12	-18	-24	-30	-36
-5	30	25	20	15	10	5	0	-5	-10	-15	-20	-25	-30
-4	24	20	16	12	8	4	0	-4	-8	-12	-16	-20	-24
-3	18	15	12	9	6	3	0	-3	-6	-9	-12	-15	-18
-2	12	10	8	6	4	2	0	-2	-4	-6	-8	-10	-12
-1	6	5	4	3	2	1	0	-1	-2	-3	-4	-5	-6
0	0	0	0	0	0	0	0	0	0	0	0	0	0
1	-6	-5	-4	-3	-2	-1	0	1	2	3	4	5	6
2	-12	-10	-8	-6	-4	-2	0	2	4	6	8	10	12
3	-18	-15	-12	-9	-6	-3	0	3	6	9	12	15	18
4	-24	-20	-16	-12	-8	-4	0	4	8	12	16	20	24
5	-30	-25	-20	-15	-10	-5	0	5	10	15	20	25	30
6	-36	-30	-24	-18	-12	-6	0	6	12	18	24	30	36

DECODE..., Page 36

This message can be decoded if you move up and to the right. If a place if filled, place the word below the last word.

LINE DESIGN, Page 37

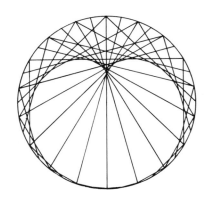

ROCK TALK, Page 38

Bob	Drums
Denny	Piano
Gil	Bass
Pete	Guitar

ARROWMATH, Page 39

SOLVE:

1) 8 → = **13**

2) 13 ↗ = **17**

3) 8 ↘ ↗ = **11**

4) 13 → ↗ ← = **17**

5) 11 → → ↗ ↗ ← = **8**

6) 12 → ↗ ↘ ↗ → ↗ ↗ ↗ ↗ ← ↘ → = **8**

7) DOES **21** → HAVE ANY MEANING? **NO**

8) DOES **4** ↑ OR ↓ HAVE ANY MEANING? **NO**

9) WHAT IS THE INVERSE OF ↗ ? ↙

10) DOES **7** → **5** HAVE A MEANING? **NO**

ARROWMATH, Page 40

SOLVE:

1) 6 → = **14**

2) 6 → → = **24**

3) 3 ↗ → = **24**

4) 15 ← ← = **11**

5) 8 ↗ → = **54**

6) 8 → ↗ = **252**

7) 11 → ↗ = **270**

8) ARE OPERATIONS ↘ AND ↗ DEFINED? **NO**

9) IN PROBLEMS 5 & 6 WAS 8 ↗ → = 8 → ↗ ? **NO**

10) IS 6 → ← EQUAL TO 6 ← → ? **NO**

11) ARE ← AND → INVERSES? **NO**

12) INVENT A MATH SYSTEM OF YOUR OWN AND TRY IT ON YOUR FRIENDS.

WHICH ONE DIFFERS?, Page 41

A) 2   D) 3

B) 1   E) 4

C) 5

COIN CAPERS, Page 42

48 coins: 24 heads, 24 tails

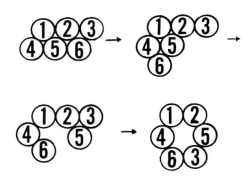

METRIC MEASURE, Page 43

1) 57mm or 5.7cm	6) 35mm or 3.5cm
2) 92mm or 9.2cm	7) 13mm or 1.3cm
3) 35mm or 3.5cm	8) 8mm or .8cm
4) 22mm or 2.2cm	9) 21mm or 2.1cm
5) 57mm or 5.7cm	

Remember, all measurement is approximate.

WHAT DO WE..., Page 44

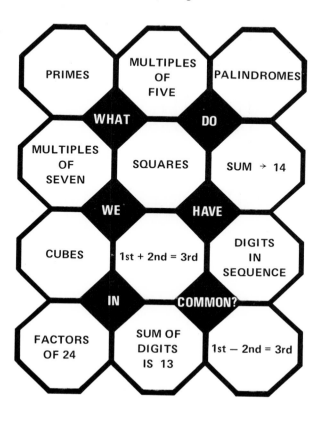

PRIMES	MULTIPLES OF FIVE	PALINDROMES
WHAT	**DO**	
MULTIPLES OF SEVEN	SQUARES	SUM → 14
WE	**HAVE**	
CUBES	1st + 2nd = 3rd	DIGITS IN SEQUENCE
IN	**COMMON?**	
FACTORS OF 24	SUM OF DIGITS IS 13	1st − 2nd = 3rd

AVERAGES, Page 45

Average Sales:	$108,500.00
Tigers' Average Score:	56
Opponents' Average Score:	47
Average Diameter:	101,830

WHICH ARE NOT CONGRUENT?, Page 46

CHANGE PROBLEM, Page 47

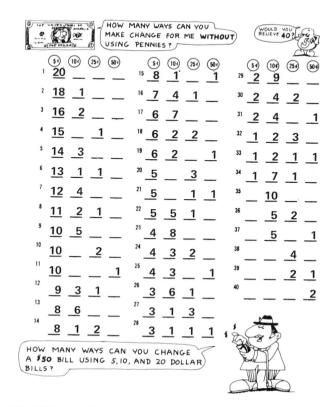

#	5¢	10¢	25¢	50¢		#	5¢	10¢	25¢	50¢		#	5¢	10¢	25¢	50¢
1	20					15	8	1		1		29	2	9		
2	18	1				16	7	4	1			30	2	4	2	
3	16	2				17	6	7				31	2	4		1
4	15		1			18	6	2	2			32	1	2	3	
5	14	3				19	6	2		1		33	1	2	1	1
6	13	1	1			20	5		3			34	1	7	1	
7	12	4				21	5		1	1		35		10		
8	11	2	1			22	5	5	1			36		5	2	
9	10	5				23	4	8				37		5		1
10	10		2			24	4	3	2			38			4	
11	10			1		25	4	3		1		39			2	1
12	9	3	1			26	3	6	1			40				2
13	8	6				27	3	1	3							
14	8	1	2			28	3	1	1	1						

TRACE A PATH TO THE CENTER, Page 48

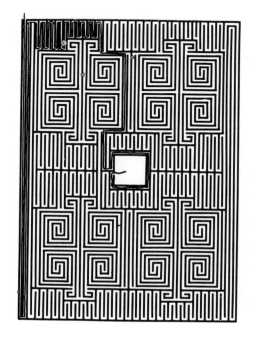

GOLDBACH'S CONJECTURE, Page 49
Answers are not unique.

PRIME FACTOR TENTS, Page 50

WHAT'S MY WORD?, Page 51

C L O T H E S P I N

A WHOLE THING, Page 52

HOW MANY?, Page 53

1) 15   3) 101
2) 27   4) 24

FRACTION TILES, Page 54

1) 1/2 − 1/6 + 1/4 = 7/12
2) 1/2 + 1/6 − 1/4 = 5/12
3) 1/2 + 1/3 + 1/6 = 1
4) 1/2 − 1/3 − 1/6 = 0
5) Can't be done.
6) 1/4 + 1/6 − 1/3 = 1/12
7) 1/2 + 1/3 − 1/6 = 2/3
8) 1/2 + 1/6 + 1/4 = 11/12

DESI AND CAROL, Page 55

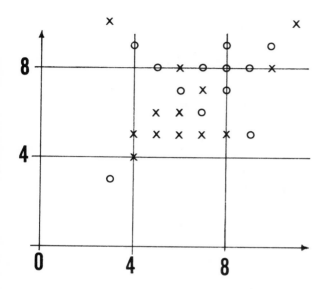

FAMOUS MATHEMATICIAN, Page 56

E U L E R

EULER LINES, Page 57

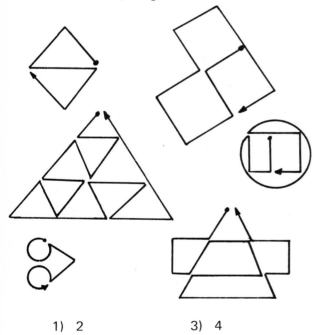

1) 2
2) 4

3) 4
4) 0

TRELLIS TWISTER, Page 62

Number 7.

WAY—OUT NUMERATION, Page 65

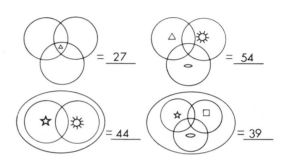

FILL IN THE SYMBOLS TO FORM THESE NUMBERS.

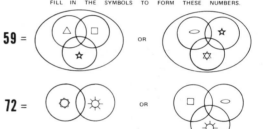

These answers may not be unique.

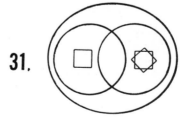

30.

31.

WAY—OUT NUMERATION, Page 65 (cont.)

32.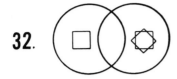

33. None

34. None

35.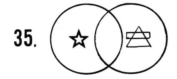

36.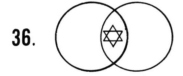

37. None

38. None

39.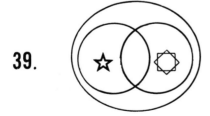

40.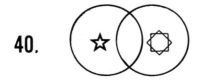

QUADRILATERAL QUEST, Page 66

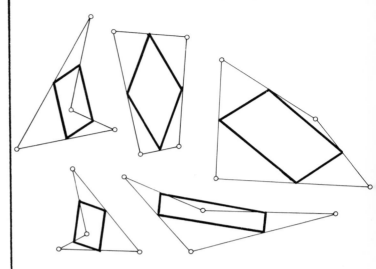

In each case a Parallelogram is formed.

NUMBER PATTERNS, Page 67

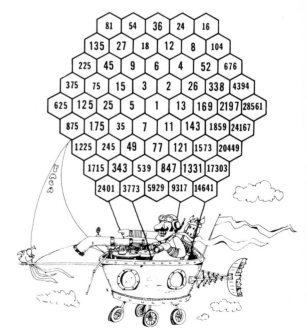

Patterns become obvious when a complete factorization is made on each number.

DECODE USING ALPHABET, Page 68

Circles which have the same center but different radii are concentric circles.

TILE TRIAL, Page 69

1) $(15 + 4 - 19) \times 10 \times 22 = 0$
2) $22 \div (15 - 4) \times 10 - 19 = 1$
3) $22 - 19 + 10 + 4 - 15 = 2$
4) $22 - 19 \div (15 - 4 - 10) = 3$
5) $22 - 19 + 15 - 10 - 4 = 4$
6) $15 - 10 \div (19 + 4 - 22) = 5$
7) $15 + 19 - 10 - 22 + 4 = 6$
8) $(15 - 4 + 10) \div (22 - 19) = 7$

Answers are not unique.

ORDER SORTER, Page 70

$Q < B < T < F < X < S < M < J < D$

T   R   I   A   N   G   L   E   S

WHICH ONE DIFFERS?, Page 72

A) 3   B) 5   C) 2   D) 3   E) 1

PLOTTING PICTURES, Page 73

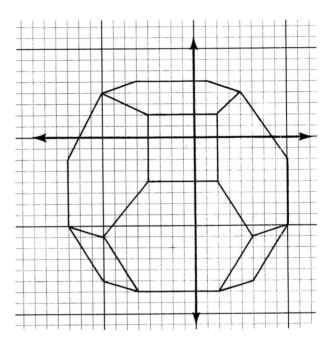

KNIGHT 'N DAZE, Page 75

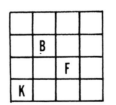

3	20	15	10	5
14	9	4	21	16
19	2	25	6	11
24	13	8	17	22
1	18	23	12	7

CONCENTRIC CIRCLES, Page 76

E and G are concentric.

CUBE FLIP AND TURN, Page 77

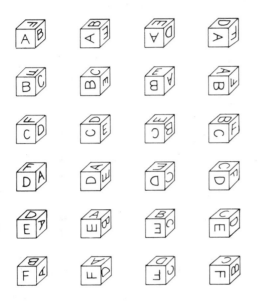

Make a model.

POLYOMINOES, Page 78

Hexaminoes — 35

Figure H can be drawn with seven line segments.

CHANZANIA, Page 79

No fair shaking the urn.

PUZZLERS, Page 80

B passes A every 12 minutes.

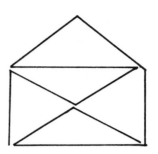

It would take about $11\frac{1}{2}$ days counting once a second, twenty-four hours a day.

HOW MANY ?, Page 81

1) 66   2) 7   3) 72
4) 12 (order of dice is not important)

TINKERTOTALS, Page 82

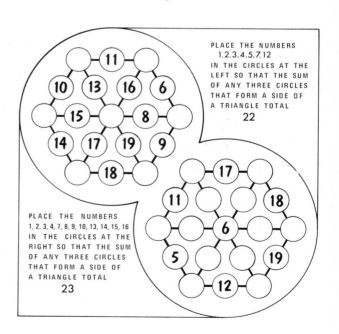

PLACE THE NUMBERS 1, 2, 3, 4, 5, 7, 12 IN THE CIRCLES AT THE LEFT SO THAT THE SUM OF ANY THREE CIRCLES THAT FORM A SIDE OF A TRIANGLE TOTAL 22

PLACE THE NUMBERS 1, 2, 3, 4, 7, 8, 9, 10, 13, 14, 15, 16 IN THE CIRCLES AT THE RIGHT SO THAT THE SUM OF ANY THREE CIRCLES THAT FORM A SIDE OF A TRIANGLE TOTAL 23

NAME GAME, Page 83

Add	Exponent	Number	Scale
Angle	Face	Numeration	Section
Apex	Fifteen	Octagon	Second
Arc	Five	One	Segment
Area	Four	Open	Seven
Arithmetic	Fourteen	Ounce	Seventeen
Axis	Fraction	Ounces	Seventeenth
Base	Gram	Parallel	Six
Bisect	Height	Parallelogram	Sixteen
Cent	Hexagon	Pattern	Sixteenth
Center	Identity	Pentagon	Slope
Centimeter	Less	Pi	Sum
Chords	Locus	Plane	Ten
Circle	Log	Plato	Tenth
Circles	Mathematics	Platonic	Tetrahedron
Cone	Measure	Probability	Third
Count	Measures	Puzzle	Thirds
Curve	Meet	Pyramid	Three
Decimal	Meter	Quart	Ton
Difference	Midpoint	Radius	Two
Divide	Minute	Ratio	Unit
Edge	Modular	Ray	Vertex
Eight	Multiple	Rectangle	Volume
Eighty	Multiplication	Regular	Weight
Eleven	Nine	Rhombus	Yard
Even	Nonagon	Round	Yards
			Zero

ONE, TWO, THREE, FOUR,..., Page 84

1) $(1 + 2 - 3) \times 4 = 0$
2) $1 \times 2 + 3 - 4 = 1$
3) $1 + 2 + 3 - 4 = 2$
4) $(1 + 2) \div 3 \times 4 = 4$
5) $(1 + 2) \times 3 - 4 = 5$
6) $1 \div 2 \times 3 \times 4 = 6$
7) $1 + 2 + 3 + 4 = 10$
8) $(1 + 2) \times 3 + 4 = 13$
9) $1 \times 2 + 3 \times 4 = 14$
10) $1 \times (2 + 3) \times 4 = 20$
11) $1 + [(2 + 3) \times 4] = 21$
12) $1 \times 2 \times 3 \times 4 = 24$

These answers are not unique.

FIND MY PATTERN, Page 85

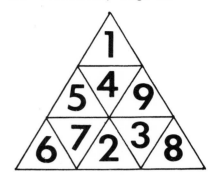

COLORING MATH MAPS, Page 89

Figure	Regions	Colors Needed
A	2	2
B	3	3
C	4	3
D	4	3
E	5	4
F	5	3
G	6	4
H	6	4
I	7	4
J	8	4

PATTERNS AND SEQUENCES, Page 91

1) 6, 12, 18, 24, 30, 36, 42
2) 3, 9, 27, 81, 243, 729, 2187
3) $\frac{1}{2}$, $\frac{1}{4}$, $\frac{1}{8}$, $\frac{1}{16}$, $\frac{1}{32}$, $\frac{1}{64}$, $\frac{1}{128}$
4) .125, .25, .375, .5, .625, .750, .875
5) 6, 4, 2, 0, -2, -4, -6
6) .1, .1, .2, .3, .5, .8, 1.3
7) 1, 1·2, 1·2·3, 24, 120, 720, 5040
8) 1_5, 4_5, 12_5, 20_5, 23_5, 31_5, 34_5
9) 1_7, 4_7, 12_7, 22_7, 34_7, 51_7, 100_7

POWER PATTERNS, Page 94

The sum of the cubes of n consecutive counting numbers equals the square of the sum of n consecutive counting numbers.

FIT THE DISCS, Page 95

$$24 \times \frac{3}{4} \times \frac{1}{6} = 3$$
$$\times$$
$$\frac{5}{6} \times 24 \times \frac{1}{4} = 5$$
$$\times \qquad \times$$
$$\frac{1}{2} \times \frac{2}{3} \times 24 = 8$$
$$= \qquad = \qquad =$$
$$10 \qquad 12 \qquad 1 \qquad \blacksquare$$

$$\frac{1}{2} + \frac{5}{12} + \frac{1}{12} = 1$$
$$+$$
$$\frac{3}{4} + \frac{5}{6} - \frac{7}{12} = 1$$
$$- \qquad - \qquad +$$
$$\frac{1}{4} + \frac{1}{4} + \frac{1}{2} = 1$$
$$= \qquad = \qquad =$$
$$1 \qquad 1 \qquad 0 \qquad \blacksquare$$

MAGIC HEXAGON, Page 97

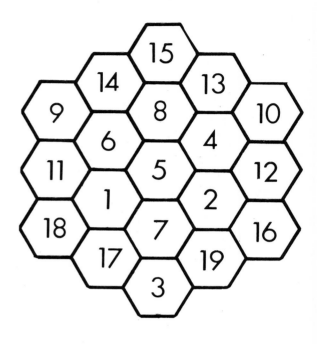

ACCURACY, Page 98
14! = 87, 178, 291, 200

HIDDEN PRODUCTS, Page 99
One-digit factors:
(2, 5)
(2, 6)
(2, 12)
(2, 15)
(2, 20)
(3, 10)
(3, 12)
(4, 3)
(4, 9)
(4, 11)
(4, 17)
(5, 6)
(5, 19)
(5, 20)
(6, 3)
(6, 17)
(7, 3)